Internet Explorer 4.0

fast & easy ™

How to Order:

For information on quantity discounts contact the publisher: Prima Publishing, P.O. Box 1260BK, Rocklin, CA 95677-1260; (916) 632-4400. On your letterhead include information concerning the intended use of the books and the number of books you wish to purchase. For individual orders, turn to the back of this book for more information.

Internet Explorer 4.0

fast & easy ™

Coletta Witherspoon

PRIMA PUBLISHING

Publisher: Matthew H. Carleson
Managing Editor: Dan J. Foster
Acquisitions Editor: Deborah F. Abshier
Development Editor: Kevin Harreld
Project Editor: Kevin Harreld
Copy Editor: Susan Christophersen
Technical Reviewer: Jeanne Balbach
Interior Design and Layout: Marian Hartsough
Cover Design: Prima Design Team
Indexer: Katherine Stimson

Microsoft is a registered trademark of Microsoft Corporation.

Important: If you have problems installing or running Microsoft Internet Explorer 4.0, notify Microsoft Corporation at (206) 635-7056. Prima Publishing cannot provide software support.

Prima Publishing and the author have attempted throughout this book to distinguish proprietary trademarks from descriptive terms by following the capitalization style used by the manufacturer.

Information contained in this book has been obtained by Prima Publishing from sources believed to be reliable. However, because of the possibility of human or mechanical error by our sources, Prima Publishing, or others, the Publisher does not guarantee the accuracy, adequacy, or completeness of any information and is not responsible for any errors or omissions or the results obtained from the use of such information. Readers should be particularly aware of the fact that the Internet is an ever-changing entity. Some facts may have changed since this book went to press.

ISBN: 0-7615-1191-1
Library of Congress Catalog Card Number: 97-67394
Printed in the United States of America

98 99 HH 10 9 8 7 6 5 4 3

To Barbara Hjelmaa

Acknowledgments

Mahalo to my many friends who have provided support and aloha over this past year. To Miss Harvey Jeanne for making my move to Hawaii so easy. To Bimbo Jones for helping me write a few chapters (and because I miss you). To Mary Lovein for being such a great e-mail buddy. And to my mom, just because she's my mom and I love her.

Many thanks to everyone at Prima for all their hard work in putting this book together. I especially want to thank Debbie Abshier for giving me this opportunity, Kevin Harreld for letting me crack jokes and start revolutions while he was trying to play taskmaster, Jeanne Balbach for making sure I kept the facts straight, and Susan Christophersen for dotting the i's and crossing the t's.

About the Author

Coletta Witherspoon is a freelance writer and editor. She has written and edited a half dozen books on the Internet, Web browsers, Web graphics, and computer networks. She has also written, edited, and produced a wide range of promotional and marketing literature, training programs, and video scripts for her corporate clients. Coletta lives in Hawaii and conducts all of her business (and a lot of her personal life) over the Internet.

Contents at a Glance

Contents

PART V
VIRTUAL CONFERENCING
WITH NETMEETING. 269

PART VII
APPENDIX 345

Introduction

This Visual Learning Guide from Prima Publishing will help you on your way to becoming an Internet egghead and simultaneously show you how to use Internet Explorer 4.0 and the other components included in the Internet Explorer suite. This book will walk you through all of the Internet Explorer suite programs, giving you step-by-step instructions along with illustrations of what you will see on your screen. This method will make it easy for you to follow a task and make sure that you achieve the desired results.

The Microsoft Internet Explorer 4.0 suite is a powerful and complete set of Internet tools. Internet Explorer and its components take you beyond simple Web browsing to new dimensions in Web technology. You will be able to experience some of the new and exciting multimedia technology that is appearing on the Internet. The Outlook Express mail and news program brings new features that will make your message system easier to use. Microsoft Chat is a fun way to take part in real-time discussion groups using comic book characters. NetMeeting will help you save money on long-distance phone bills and is a great tool for telecommuters. FrontPage Express can help make your presence on the Internet possible.

WHO SHOULD READ THIS BOOK?

As you thumb through this book, you may think that it is just for beginners because of the easy-to-follow directions and generous use of illustrations. But it is also the perfect tool for those who are familiar with the Internet and Web browsing and want to get up to speed with Internet Explorer 4.0 quickly. You may need to read all of the individual chapters in a section of the book to master its subject matter, or you may need only certain chapters to fill in the gaps in your existing knowledge. This book is structured to support the procedure that suits you best.

This book also makes a great reference tool. With all of the software available today and the myriad of software programs that you may use in your personal and business life, sometimes you just need a quick reminder of how to use a program to perform different tasks. You can easily look up a task without having to wade through pages of descriptions, definitions, and reference material.

HELPFUL HINTS TO INCREASE YOUR SKILLS

The use of easy-to-follow steps and detailed illustrations helps you learn quickly. This book also contains other elements that provide additional information to enhance your learning experience:

✦ **Tips** provide you with helpful hints to make your job easier.

✦ **Notes** offer additional information about a task or feature.

Also, the appendix shows you how to find help from inside a program or from the Internet. By taking advantage of all the help available to you, you can go from being a newbie to an egghead, or from being an egghead to a wizard.

The Internet Explorer 4.0 Visual Learning Guide is so easy to use that you should be ready to surf the Internet with Internet Explorer in practically no time. So have a good time!

PART I
Getting Internet Explorer Up and Running

plor
el

f the we

pecial D
Bringing Y

ush technology"
own—but what e
how Microsoft Int
push technology t
new channels tha

1 Getting Started with Internet Explorer

Welcome to a new world of technology. You're just in time to join the party. Life on the Internet is becoming more exciting every day, and the variety of content is growing constantly. Information is being delivered to you at faster speeds, and new methods of delivering that content are being developed. IE 4.0 will put you in the driver's seat and let you control how your computer accesses the Internet. In this chapter, you'll learn how to:

✦ Download Internet Explorer from the Internet

✦ Install Internet Explorer on your computer

✦ Add additional components to the Internet Explorer suite

DOWNLOADING INTERNET EXPLORER

When you download Internet Explorer, it gives you three options: minimal, standard, or full installation. This book assumes that you downloaded the full installation. If you downloaded only the standard installation, you can always return to the Microsoft Web site and download any additional components that you feel will be useful. This section will walk you through the process of downloading Internet Explorer from the Microsoft Web site.

1. **Type** the **address** of the Internet Explorer 4.0 Web site located at http://www. microsoft.com/ie/ie40. The Internet Explorer Web page will begin to download.

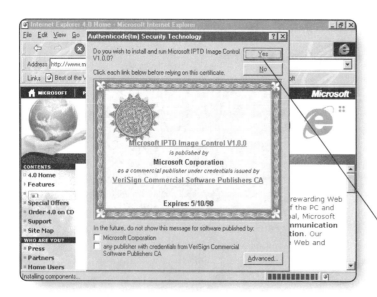

NOTE

If this is the first time that you have visited this site, a series of security dialog boxes will open. You will need these controls to display the Internet Explorer 4.0 Web site and download the Internet Explorer programs.

2. **Click** on **Yes**. The page will continue to download and another security dialog box will appear.

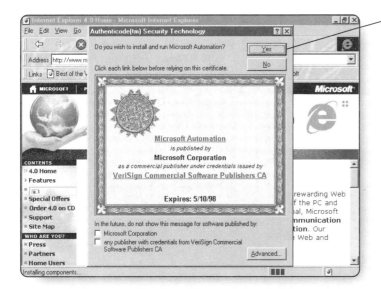

3. **Click** on **Yes**. The Web page will continue to download and another security dialog box will open.

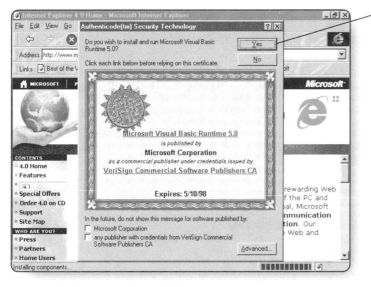

4. **Click** on **Yes**. The Internet Explorer 4.0 Web page will appear.

5. Click on the **Download Internet Explorer 4.0 button**. The Internet Explorer Download page will appear.

6. Press and **hold** the **mouse button** on the **scroll bar** and **drag it** until you see the Download Internet Explorer 4.0 link.

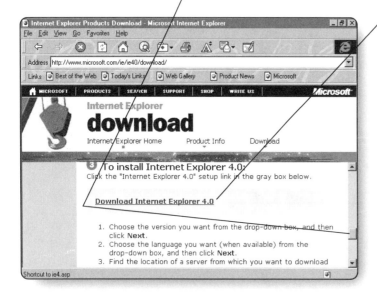

7. Click on the **Download Internet Explorer 4.0 link**. Another download page will appear.

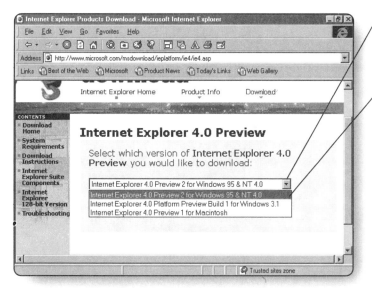

8. **Click** on the **down arrow** (▼) next to the list box. A drop-down list will appear.

9. **Click** on the **operating system** that your computer uses. The operating system will be selected.

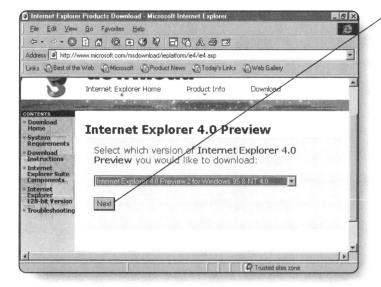

10. **Click** on Next. Another download page will appear.

NOTE

Depending on how you have the security settings of your browser set up, you may see a series of security dialog boxes that tell you that you are sending information over the Internet. If this happens, click on Yes. If you click on No, you will not be able to download the Internet Explorer program.

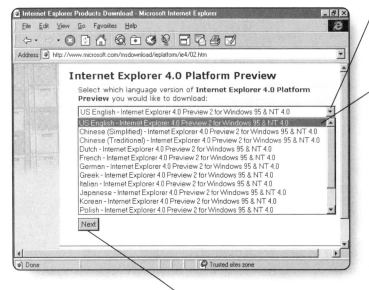

11. **Click** on the **down arrow** (▼) next to the list box. A drop-down list will appear.

12. **Click** on the **language** that you want. The language will be selected.

NOTE

The languages for your operating system and Internet Explorer must match.

13. **Click** on **Next**. A list of download sites will appear.

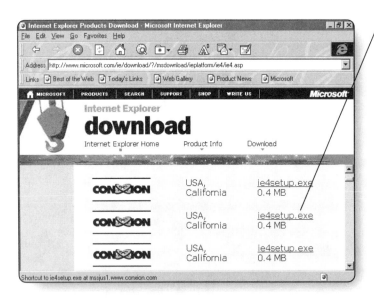

14. **Click** on the **file** that corresponds to the download site that you find to be the closest to your geographic location. A dialog box will open.

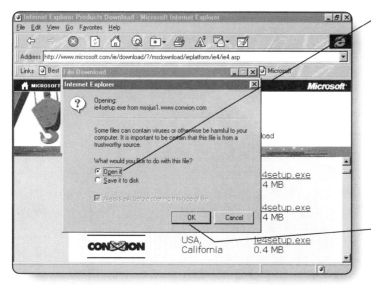

15. **Click** on the **Open it option button** to open the setup file after it is downloaded. The option will be selected.

16. **Click** on **OK**. The setup file will begin to download.

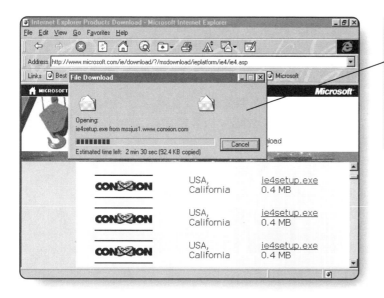

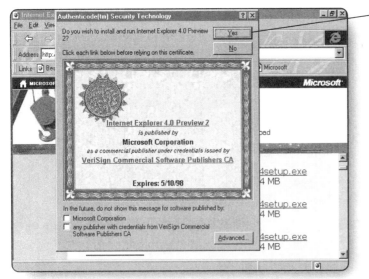

17. **Click** on **Yes** after the file has finished downloading and a security dialog box has appeared. The Internet Explorer 4.0 Active Setup Wizard will begin.

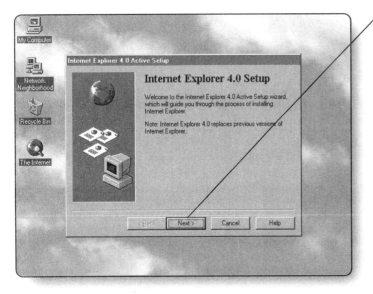

18. **Click** on **Next**. The License Agreement will appear.

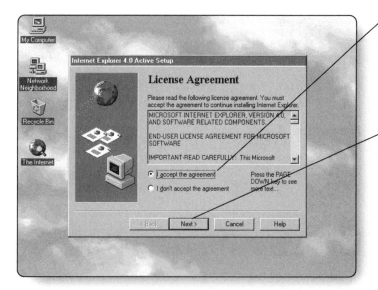

19. Read the **License Agreement** and **click** on the **option button** that says you accept the agreement. The option will be selected.

20. Click on Next. The Installation options will appear.

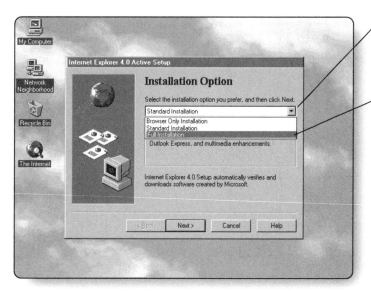

21. Click on the **down arrow** (▼) next to the list box. A drop-down list will appear.

22. Click on an **installation type**. The installation type will be selected.

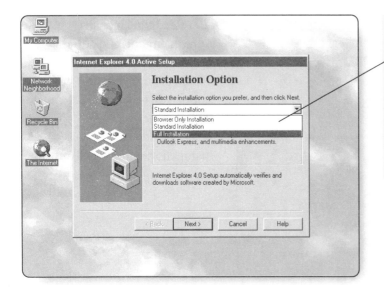

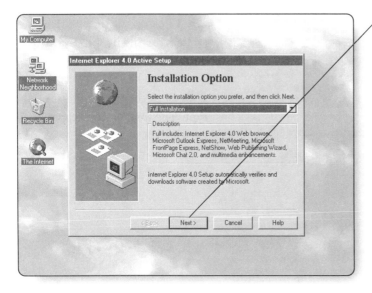

23. **Click** on **Next**. The Windows Desktop Update option will appear.

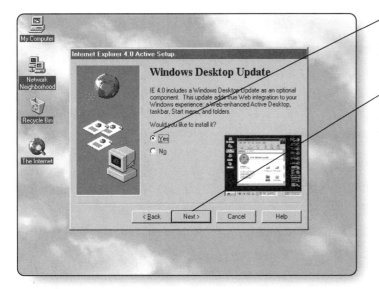

24. Click on the **option to install the Windows Desktop.** The option will be selected.

25. Click on Next. The Installation Folder options will appear.

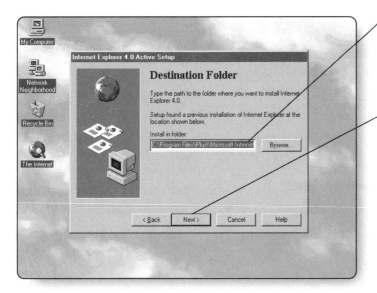

26. Type the **drive designation and folder** to which you want Internet Explorer and its components installed.

27. Click on Next.

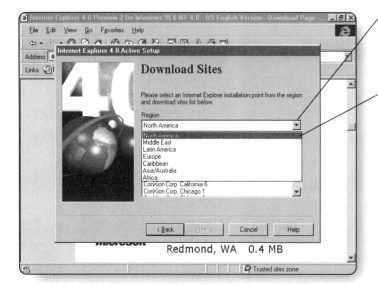

28. **Click** on the **down arrow** (▼) next to the region list box. A drop-down list will appear.

29. **Click** on the **region** where you live. Your region will be selected.

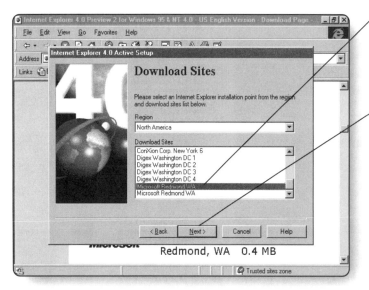

30. **Click** on a **download site** that is nearest to your geographical location. The download site will be selected.

31. **Click** on **Next**. The Internet Explorer setup will begin preparing to download the program to your computer. Wait while the setup program prepares to begin the download process. The download status screen will appear.

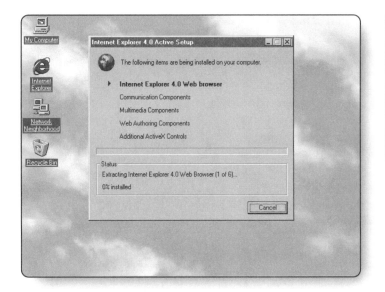

NOTE

It's going to be a long wait while the installation files download to your computer. Grab a cup of coffee and a doughnut, put your feet up, and relax.

TIP

If you have to cancel the download or if you are disconnected from the Internet, look for the ie4setup.exe file on your computer and double-click on it. The download process will begin where you left off.

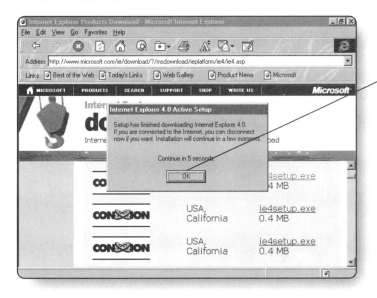

INSTALLING INTERNET EXPLORER

After a long wait, you are now ready to install the program. The following steps will lead you through the remainder of the installation process.

1. Click on **OK** when the installation files have finished downloading and a dialog box has appeared. The Installation dialog box will then open. Wait while Internet Explorer installs on your computer. When the installation is complete, another dialog box will open.

NOTE

When the installation process is complete, make sure that your Internet connection is turned off and that all programs are closed.

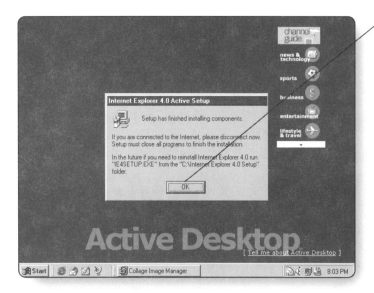

2. **Click** on **OK**. Your computer will restart.

NOTE

When the computer restarts, you will see a series of dialog boxes telling you that shortcuts are being updated and program files are being updated. Again, be patient; this update will take a few minutes. When the installation is complete, you will be back in control of your computer again.

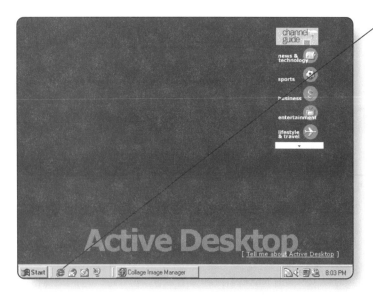

3. **Click** on the **Internet Explorer 4.0 icon**. You will be able to register your copy of Internet Explorer.

ADDING INTERNET EXPLORER COMPONENTS

The list of available additional software components is vast. These software components are what give Internet Explorer its power. Several core components add functionality beyond the basic browser, such as electronic mail, chat, conferencing, and FTP. Other components add functionality to the browser, such as the VRML Viewer, sound packs, and NetShow.

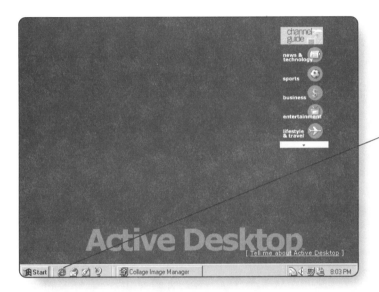

1. **Click** on **The Internet icon** on your desktop.

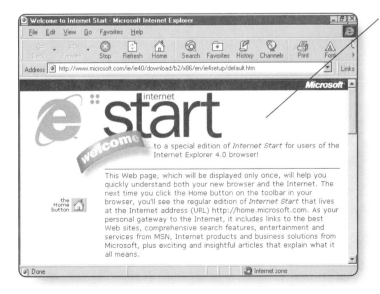

Internet Explorer 4.0 will open and the Welcome to Internet Start page will appear.

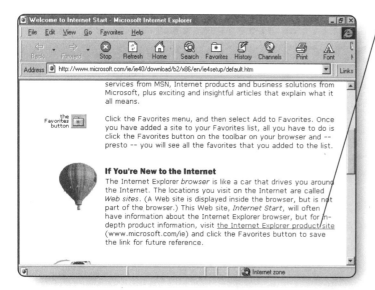

2. Scroll down the page and click on the Internet Explorer Product Site hyperlink. The Internet Explorer Home page will appear.

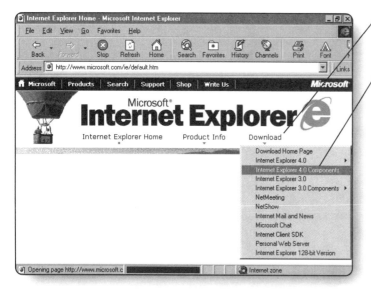

3. Click on the Download link. A menu will appear.

4. Click on Internet Explorer 4.0 Components. The Internet Explorer Products Download page will appear.

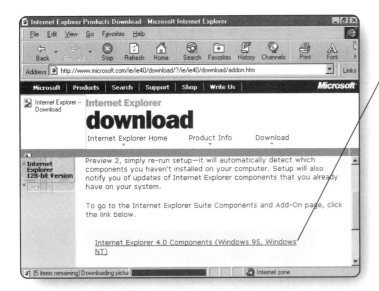

5. **Scroll down** the **page** until you see the Components link.

6. **Click** on the **Components link**. The Components page will begin to download. The Components page will take a couple of minutes to initialize. Wait until the page appears and a dialog box opens.

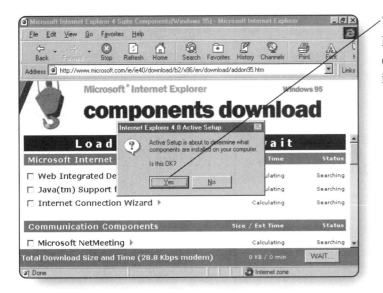

7. **Click** on **Yes**. Internet Explorer will determine which components are already installed and which aren't.

8. **Click** on the **components** that you want to install. A ✔ will appear in the boxes next to the components you selected.

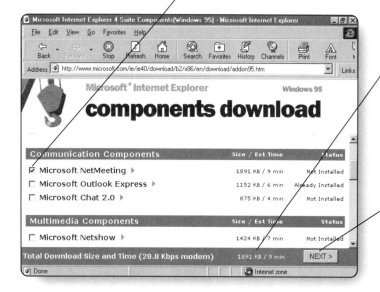

9. **Click** on **Next**. Another download page will appear.

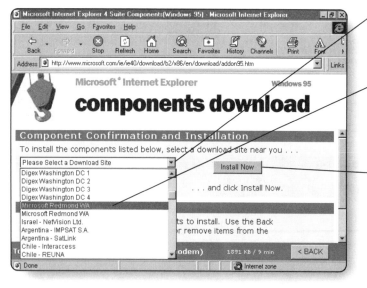

10. **Click** on the **down arrow** (▼) next to the list box. A list of download sites will appear.

11. **Click** on the **download site** that is closest to your geographical location. The site will be selected.

12. **Click** on **Install Now**. The Active Setup dialog box will open. Wait while the components that you selected are downloaded to your computer. It may be time to refresh that cup of coffee.

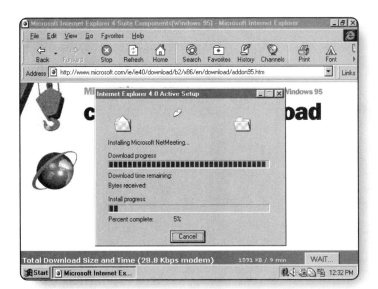

NOTE

When the download is complete, the components will be installed. This will be a relatively short wait. When the installation is complete, a dialog box will open.

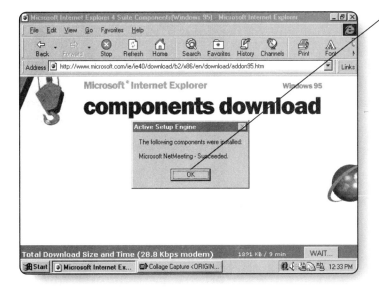

13. **Click** on **OK**. The Components page will appear.

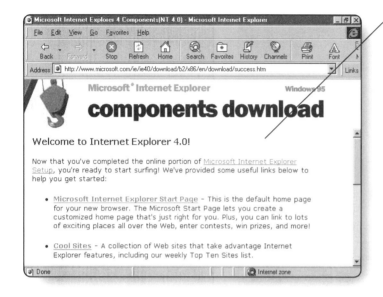

14. Click on **any link** to find out more about Internet Explorer and its components. The link will be selected. This is a great place to begin exploring!

2 Starting and Exiting Programs

Even if you've used previous versions of Internet Explorer, you will find something new in version 4.0. Internet Explorer can be installed with a number of other Internet applications to make up the Internet Explorer suite. As with other software suites, the Internet Explorer suite programs can be used separately or in conjunction with each other. Just because there are several programs to learn, this does not have to be an overwhelming task. The programs in the Internet Explorer suite share a number of common elements, which gives you a familiar place to start with each new program. In this chapter, you'll learn how to:

✦ **Start Internet Explorer suite programs**

✦ **Start Internet Explorer suite programs from other suite programs**

✦ **Identify the screen elements that are common to the Internet Explorer suite programs**

✦ **Use menus and toolbars**

✦ **Exit Internet Explorer suite programs**

STARTING PROGRAMS

There are several methods for starting Internet Explorer suite programs. This section shows you how to start programs using each method.

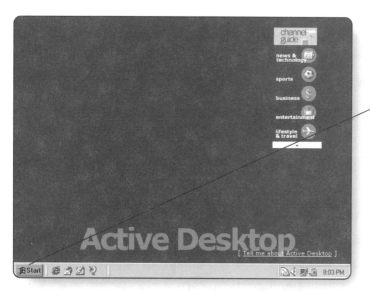

Starting a Program from the Start Menu

1. Click on the **Start button** on the Windows taskbar. The Start Menu will appear.

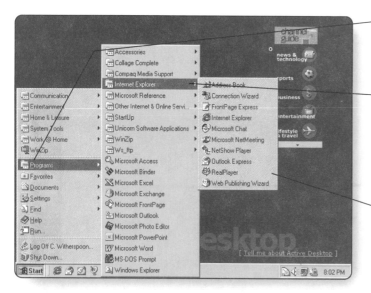

2. Move the **mouse pointer** to Programs. The Programs menu will appear.

3. Move the **mouse pointer** to the right to Internet Explorer. Another menu that lists the programs in the suite will appear.

4. Click on the **name** of the program you want to open. The program will open.

Starting a Program from the Windows Taskbar

Internet Explorer changes the way your Windows taskbar looks. When the Internet Explorer suite is installed, icons for the browser and Outlook Express are added to the taskbar.

1a. **Click** on the **Browser button**. The Internet Explorer browser will open.

OR

1b. **Click** on the **Outlook Express button.** The Outlook Express mail and news program will open.

TIP

If you are unsure which button is which, just hold the mouse pointer over the button, and a tool tip will appear with the name of the button.

Starting a Program from Within Another Program

Internet Explorer, Outlook Express, and NetMeeting all have the ability to open other programs with a menu command.

1. **Click** on **Go**. The Go menu will appear.

NOTE

You'll learn more about each of
these programs later in the book.

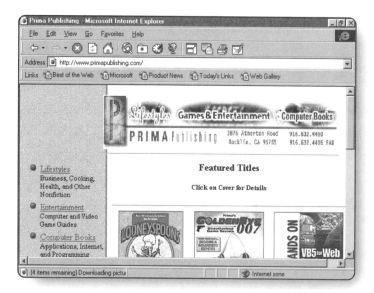

2. **Choose** from the following
options on the Go menu:

✦ **Click** on **Home Page.** Internet
Explorer will start with your
home page displayed.

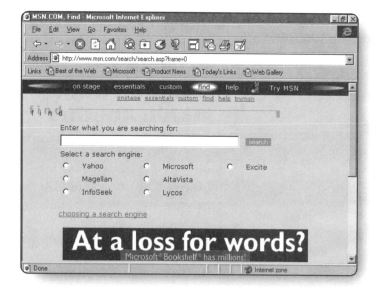

✦ **Click** on **Search the Web.**
Internet Explorer will start
with the search page
displayed.

✦ **Click** on **Best of the Web.**
Internet Explorer will start
with a list of what Microsoft
feels are the best Web pages
displayed.

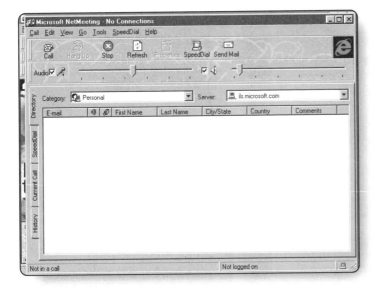

✦ **Click** on **Internet Call.**
NetMeeting will start.

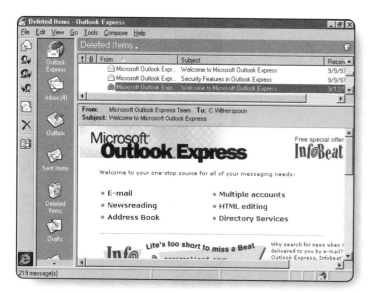

✦ **Click** on **Mail**. Outlook Express will start so that you can send and receive e-mail.

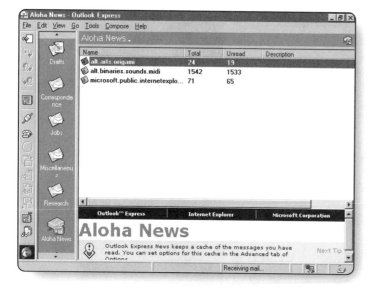

✦ **Click** on **News**. Outlook Express will start so that you can work with newsgroups.

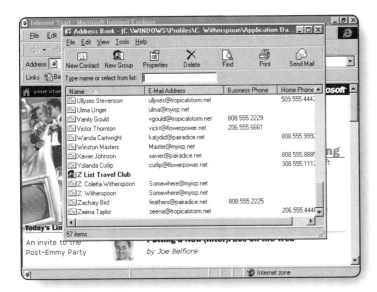

✦ **Click** on **Address Book**. The Windows Address Book will open.

IDENTIFYING COMMON SCREEN ELEMENTS

When you look at the screens for the various Internet Explorer suite programs, it may seem like you will never figure out how all these programs work. Don't be discouraged. All of the Internet Explorer suite programs use the same familiar Windows interface.

Using Menus

Menus contain all of the functions that a program can perform. Each program contains several menus. Each menu contains a number of related commands.

If a menu command is grayed out, that means that the command is not available. You may need to open a document or perform a certain function to use the grayed out command.

When a menu command is followed by an ellipsis, it means that a dialog box will appear if that command is selected.

When a right-pointing arrowhead follows a menu command, it means another menu will appear when the mouse pointer is moved over the command.

1. **Place** the **mouse pointer** over a menu command with a right-pointing arrowhead. A second menu will appear.

2. **Move** the **mouse pointer** to the right over a command on the second menu. The command will be highlighted.

3. **Click** on the **command**. The command will be executed.

Using Dialog Boxes

Dialog boxes let you perform a variety of functions, such as saving files and setting preferences. Dialog boxes contain elements such as tabs that group several dialog boxes into one, buttons that display secondary dialog boxes, and drop-down boxes that let you select a number of predefined options.

1. **Click** on **File**. The File menu will appear.

2. **Click** on **Print**. The Print dialog box will open. You will notice the following:

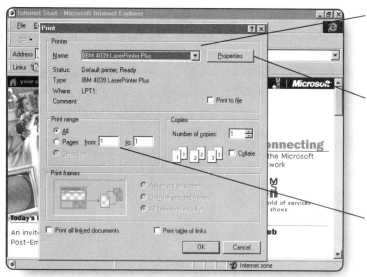

♦ The Printer section lists information about the default printer that will be used to print the document.

♦ The Properties button will display a second dialog box where you can change options such as page orientation and print resolution.

♦ The Print Range section will specify which pages are printed.

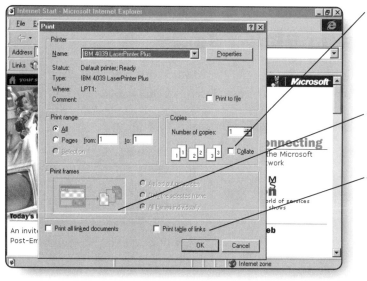

♦ The Copies section will specify how many copies of each page will be printed and if the pages should be collated.

♦ The Print Frames section is used when you print a Web page that includes frames.

♦ The Linked Documents section is used when you print a Web page that contains hyperlinks.

NOTE

If you want to close a dialog box without accepting any of the changes you have made, click on the Cancel button.

Using Toolbars

The toolbars in the Internet Explorer suite programs contain a number of buttons. These buttons can be thought of as shortcuts to the more commonly used menu commands.

1. **Place** the **mouse pointer** over a button. A tool tip will appear telling you what function the button performs.

2. **Click** on the **button**. The command associated with the button will be executed.

NOTE

Some buttons contain a down arrow. When you click on one of these down arrows, a drop-down menu will appear. Move your mouse arrow over a command from this menu and click.

Using Scroll Bars

You will find two types of scroll bars in Internet Explorer suite programs: vertical scroll bars and horizontal scroll bars.

✦ Click on the arrow at either end of the vertical or horizontal scroll bar. This will move you through the document line by line.

✦ Place the mouse pointer over the box located in the scroll bar. Press and hold the mouse button and drag the box. Release the mouse button when you are at the desired place in the document. This allows you to move to the place you want in the document.

✦ Place the mouse pointer inside the scroll bar and click the mouse button. This moves you through the document one screen at a time.

EXITING PROGRAMS

As is the case with all Windows programs, you have two options for closing Internet Explorer suite programs.

Exiting a Program from the File Menu

1. **Click** on **File**. The File menu will appear.

2. **Click** on **Close**. The program will close.

Exiting a Program from the Title Bar

1. **Click** on the **Close button** ([X]) in the upper right corner of the program window. The program will close.

TIP

When you have closed the Internet Explorer suite programs and are finished with your Internet session, remember to disconnect from your ISP.

3 Choosing Commands

The Internet Explorer suite programs share a number of similarities. The programs not only execute commands in the same ways but also perform identical commands. This chapter shows you how to use commands that are common to all of the Internet Explorer suite programs, such as saving and printing. You will discover different methods of executing these programs: by use of a menu, a button, or a right-click. In this chapter, you'll learn how to:

✦ Save and print files, messages, and Web pages

✦ Perform basic editing tasks

✦ Set up toolbars to fit the way you work

✦ Send files

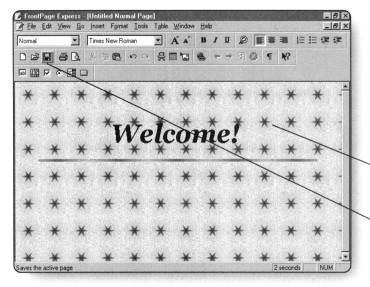

SAVING FILES

The easiest way to save a file is to use the Save button. If you prefer to be adventurous, you can look for the Save command in the File menu.

1. **Display** the **page** you want to save.

2. **Click** on the **Save button**. The Save As dialog box will open.

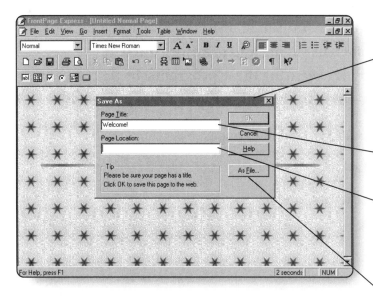

NOTE

FrontPage Express is slightly different in the way it saves files. It adds an extra dialog box to the save process.

3. **Type** a **title** for the page in the Page Title: text box.

4. **Clear** the **Page Location:** text box. (This is not needed if you are saving the file to your computer.)

5. **Click** on **As File**. The Save As File dialog box will open.

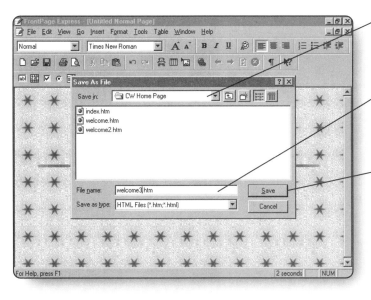

6. **Select** the **directory** in which you want to save the file. The directory will be selected.

7. **Type** a **name** for the file. The program that you are using will automatically choose a file type.

8. **Click** on **Save**. The file will be stored in the designated directory on your computer.

Making Copies of Your Files

When you have a file of which you want to keep a duplicate, or that you want to save under a different name, you will use the Save As command from the file menu.

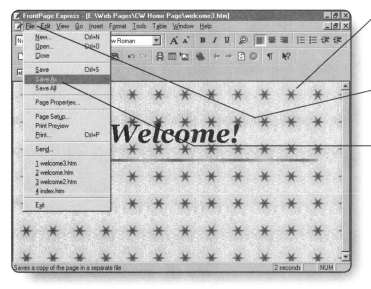

1. **Display** the **file** of which you want to make the duplicate copy.

2. **Click** on **File**. The File menu will appear.

3. **Click** on **Save As**. The Save As dialog box will open.

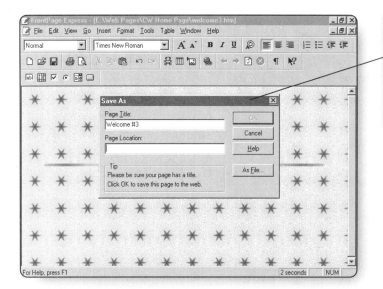

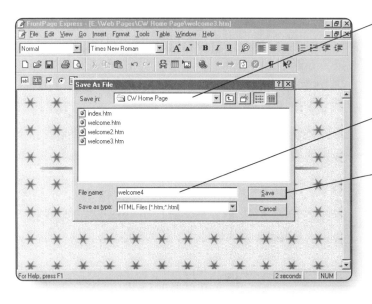

4. Click on the **directory** in which you want to save the duplicate file. The directory will be selected.

5. Type a **new name** for the file in the File name: text box.

6. Click on Save. A duplicate copy of the file will be saved on your computer in the directory that you specified.

Saving Web Page Elements

If you are looking for a way to save elements from a Web page, try the right-click method.

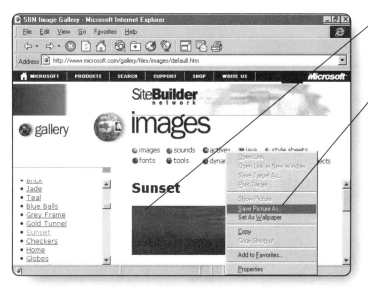

1. Right-click on the **image** that you want to save. A shortcut menu will appear.

2. Click on **Save Picture As**. The Save Picture dialog box will open.

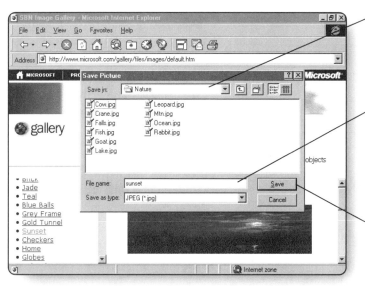

3. Click on the **directory** in which you want the file to be saved on your computer. The directory will be selected.

4. Type a **name** for the image. If this field is already filled in, you may leave the filename the same, or you can give the file a different name.

5. Click on **Save**. The image will be saved to your computer in the directory specified.

PRINTING FILES

Several steps are involved in printing files. You can use Print Preview to see what the file will look like on paper. You can use Page Setup to change the page layout settings if you don't like the way the file fits on the page. And finally, you can commit your file to paper by using the Print button.

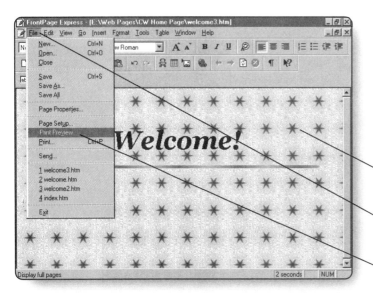

Previewing Your Files

Print Preview is a great place to go if you want to see what your file will look like before you commit it to paper.

1. Open the **file** you want to print.

2. Click on **File**. The File menu will appear.

3. Click on **Print Preview**. The file will appear in the Print Preview screen. This is how it will look after it has printed.

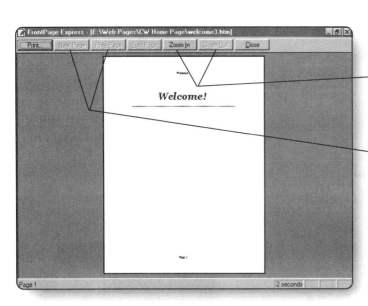

4. Click on **Zoom In** and **Zoom Out**. The file will display in different sizes.

5. Click on **Next Page** or **Prev Page** (if you have a multiple-page file). Another page in the file will appear.

6. Click on **Print**. The file will be sent to the printer.

7. Click on **Two Page** (if you have a multiple page file). The odd and even numbered pages will appear side by side.

8. Click on **Close**. The Print Preview screen will close and you will return to the program.

Changing the Page Layout Settings

If you don't like the way your file appears on the page, you can easily change some of its layout settings.

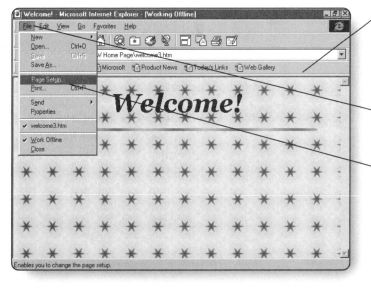

1. Open the **page** to which you want to make changes concerning the page layout setting.

2. Click on **File**. The File menu will appear.

3. Click on **Page Setup**. The Page Setup dialog box will open.

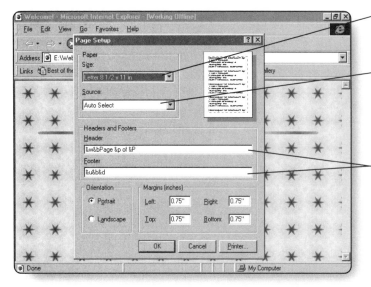

4. Select the correct **paper size** from the drop-down box.

5. Select the **source tray** where the printer needs to look for the paper on which you want the file to print.

6. Add **header** and **footer information** to the printed page.

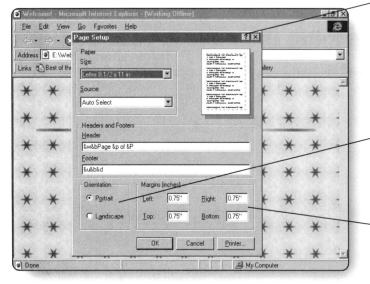

TIP

Click on the question mark (**?**), and then click on the Headers and Footers section. A screen tip with the header and footer codes and a description will appear.

7. Click on **Portrait** or **Landscape**. The paper orientation will be adjusted accordingly.

8. Click in the **Margins** fields and **type** a **new value** for the margins.

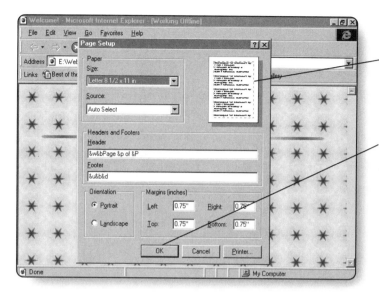

NOTE

The thumbnail view shows how the page will look with the settings that you use.

9. Click on **OK**. Your new settings will be applied.

NOTE

To see these new settings, use the Print Preview command. If you are happy with these settings, click on the Print button. Your file will be on its way to the printer.

EDITING

Editing is making changes to the text and other elements in a file. The easiest way to perform most editing tasks is by using keyboard shortcuts.

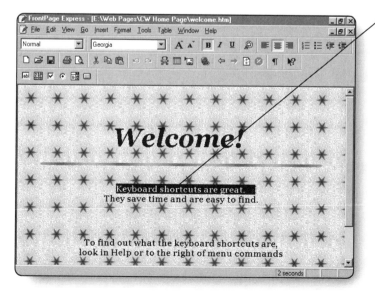

1. Select the **text** that you want to move or copy. A black box will appear around the text.

2a. Press Ctrl+X on the keyboard to move the text. The text will disappear and will be placed in the Windows clipboard.

OR

2b. Press Ctrl+C on the keyboard to copy the text. The text will stay and a copy of it will be placed in the Windows clipboard.

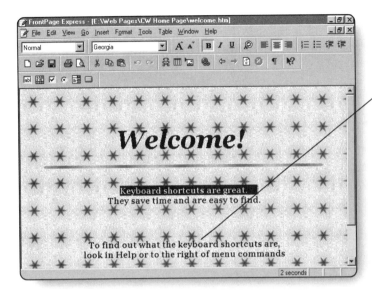

3. **Click** on the **place** in the file where you want to insert the text.

4. **Press Ctrl+V** on the keyboard. The text contained in the Windows clipboard will be placed in the file where you have indicated.

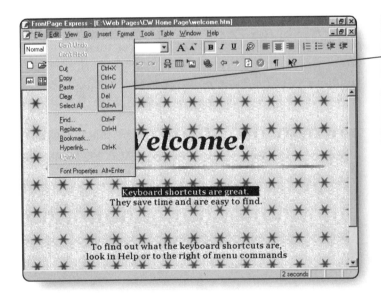

NOTE

Keyboard shortcuts can be found by searching through the program's help files or by looking at the right side of the Edit menu list.

FINDING REFERENCES

Many programs contain a Find command. The Find command allows you to find certain words on a page, messages in your inbox, or messages in a newsgroup.

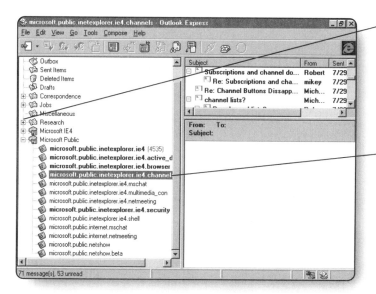

1a. Click on the **plus sign** next to the news server that contains the newsgroup you want to search. The list of subscribed newsgroups will appear.

OR

1b. Click on the **newsgroup** in which you want to find a message. The list of messages posted to the newsgroup will appear.

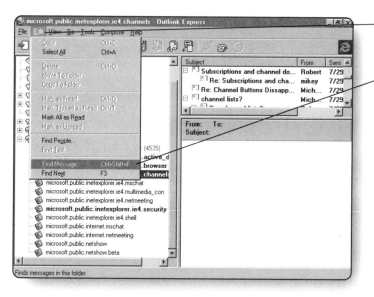

2. Click on **Edit**. The Edit menu will appear.

3. Click on **Find Message**. The Find Message dialog box will open.

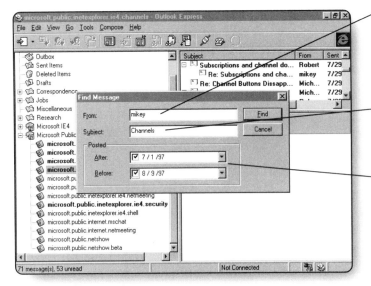

4. **Type** the **name** of the originator of the message that you are trying to find in the From: text box.

5. **Type** the **subject** of the message you are trying to find in the Subject: text box.

6. **Type** a **date range** in the After: and Before: text boxes during which you remember seeing the message.

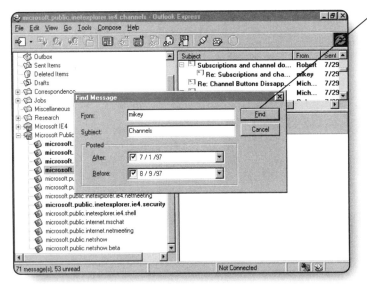

7. **Click** on the **Find button**. The program will search for any references that match your Find criteria. Found messages will be displayed in the program window and will be highlighted.

WORKING WITH TOOLBARS

Most of the Internet Explorer suite programs allow you to decide which toolbars you want to see on the program's screen and how you want to display them.

Displaying Toolbars

It's easy to show and hide toolbars. It's only a right-click away. If you want another method of choosing toolbars, try the View menu.

1. Right-click on an **empty area** of the menu bar or any toolbar. A shortcut menu will appear. Notice the following:

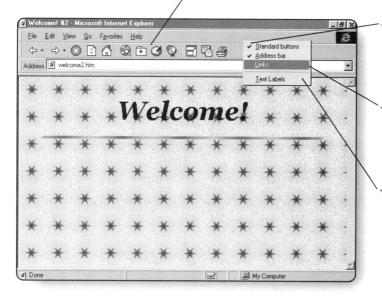

✦ A ✔ next to a menu item means that the toolbar is displayed. To hide the toolbar, click on its menu command.

✦ An item that does not have a ✔ next to it is not displayed. To display the toolbar, click on its menu command.

✦ If you want to see the descriptions of the toolbar buttons on the toolbar, make sure there is a ✔ next to Text Labels.

Customizing Toolbars

A number of Internet Explorer suite programs allow you to change the buttons that appear on a toolbar, as well as the order in which they appear.

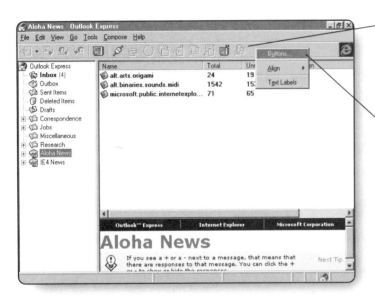

1. **Right-click** on the **toolbar** to which you want to make changes. A shortcut menu will appear.

2. **Click** on **Buttons**. The Customize Toolbar dialog box will open.

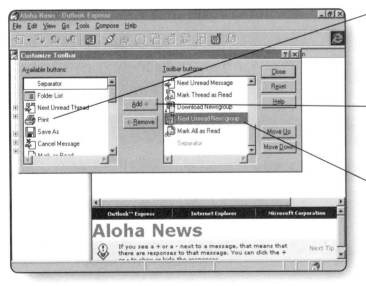

3. **Click** on a **button** in the Available buttons: list box that you want to add to your toolbar. The button will be selected.

4. **Click** on **Add**. The button will appear in the Toolbar buttons: list box.

5. **Click** on a **button** in the Toolbar buttons: list box that you want to remove from your toolbar. The button will be selected.

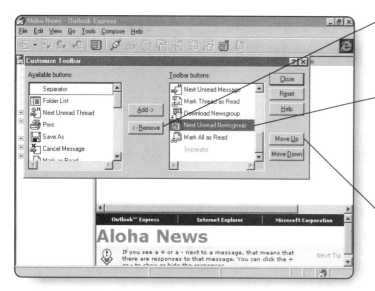

6. **Click** on **Remove**. The button will be removed and will appear in the Available buttons: list box.

7. **Click** on a **button** in the Toolbar buttons: list box that you want to move to a different order on the toolbar. The button will be selected.

8. **Click** on **Move Up**. The button will move up one place in the Toolbar buttons: list box. This corresponds to moving the button to the left on the toolbar.

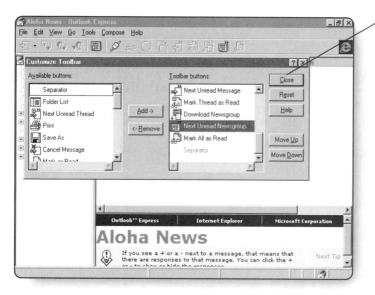

9. **Click** on **Close**. Your changes will be applied and the toolbar will appear with your changes made.

SENDING FILES AND DOCUMENTS

You don't always have to open your mail program to send someone a message. Here are a few quick shortcuts.

Forwarding Messages to Others

As you lurk through the various newsgroups, you may come across some valuable information that will help a friend solve a computer problem. Instead of telling your friend about the newsgroup, you can e-mail the newsgroup messages to your friend.

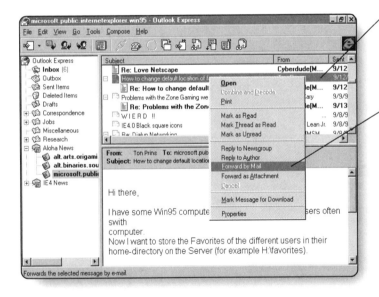

1. **Right-click** on the **message** that you want to send to someone else. A shortcut menu will appear.

2. **Click** on **Forward by Mail**. A message dialog box will open with the original message displayed in the message pane.

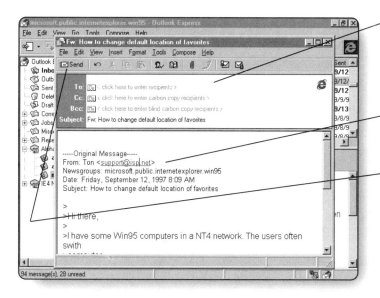

3. Type the **e-mail address** in the To: area of the person to whom you want to send the message.

4. Type in a **message** in the message area.

5. Click on the **Send button**. Your message will be on its way to its recipient.

E-mailing Web Pages

When you find a Web page that would interest a friend or colleague, you can send them more than just the URL address for the page. You can send them the whole Web page: graphics, links, and everything.

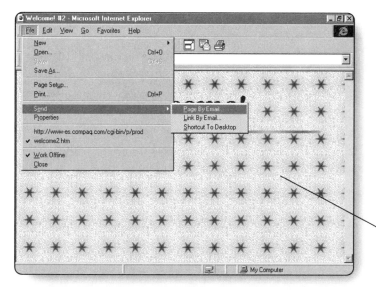

1. Open the **file** that you want to send to someone else.

2. **Click** on **File**. The File menu will appear.

3. **Click** on **Send**. A cascading menu will appear.

4. **Click** on **Page By Email**. A message dialog box will open.

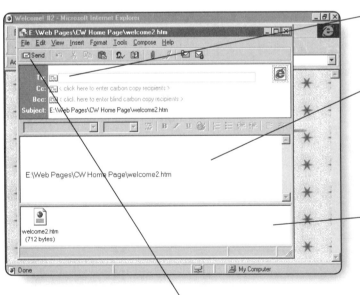

5. **Type** the **e-mail address** in the To: area of the person to whom you want to send the file.

6. **Type** a **message** in the message area so that your recipient knows to what the attachment pertains.

NOTE

The file shows as an attachment at the bottom of the message dialog box.

7. **Click** on the **Send button**. Your message will be on its way to the recipient.

PART I REVIEW QUESTIONS

1. Can you choose the Internet Explorer suite components you can download and install on your computer? *See "Downloading Internet Explorer" in Chapter 1.*

2. How do you restart the Active Setup if you are disconnected from the Internet while downloading Internet Explorer? *See "Downloading Internet Explorer" in Chapter 1.*

3. Can you add components to the Internet Explorer suite even if you didn't select them during the initial installation of Internet Explorer? *See "Adding Internet Explorer Components" in Chapter 1.*

4. What are the three different ways that you can open Internet Explorer suite programs? *See "Starting Programs" in Chapter 2.*

5. What is a quick and easy way to find out what command a toolbar button performs? *See "Using Toolbars" in Chapter 2.*

6. What are the two different ways that you can exit Internet Explorer suite programs? *See "Exiting Programs" in Chapter 2.*

7. How can you create a duplicate copy of a file? *See "Saving Files" in Chapter 3.*

8. Is it possible to see what a file will look like on paper before it is sent to your printer? *See "Printing Files" in Chapter 3.*

9. How do you change a file's layout settings? *See "Printing Files" in Chapter 3.*

10. How can you tell if you have attached a document to an e-mail message? *See "Sending Files and Documents" in Chapter 3.*

PART II

Surfing the Internet with Internet Explorer

4

What's on the Internet Explorer Screen

In the previous chapter you learned how to use menus, buttons, and commands that are common to Internet Explorer suite programs. This chapter looks at tools that are unique to the Internet Explorer browser. You are introduced to Internet Explorer's features through a guided visual tour. This visual tour will help you get familiar with the program before you dive into those waves and surf the Internet. In this chapter, you'll learn how to:

✦ Navigate between Web pages using menu commands and toolbar buttons

✦ Add the Explorer Bar to the browser window

✦ Set viewing options

✦ Access Web pages using the Address box

✦ Identify the navigation elements in the browser window

UNDERSTANDING MENU COMMANDS

This section will give you a basic understanding of some of the menu commands that are unique to Internet Explorer.

Accessing Visited Web Pages

You may wish to return to a certain Web page after surfing different sites on the Internet. Or, you may want to view Web pages offline.

1. **Click** on **File**. The File menu will appear.

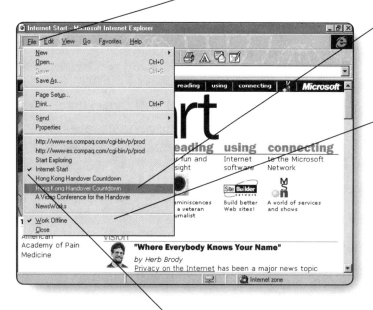

2. **Click** on an **item** in the Recent History list. The Web page will appear in the browser window.

3. **Click** on **Work Offline**. When this menu command is checked, Internet Explorer will retrieve requested Web pages from the History folder.

NOTE

Use the Recent History list to return to a site you have visited during your current Internet session. The page displayed in the browser window will have a ✔ next to it in the Recent History list.

Editing a Web Page

Is there a Web page that you want to use as a template to design your own Web page? Internet Explorer makes it easy to import that Web page into your favorite HTML editor.

1. Click on **Edit**. The Edit menu will appear.

2. Click on **Page**. Your default HTML editor will start and the Web page displayed in the browser window will be loaded into the editor so that you can make changes to the Web page.

NOTE

Learn more about editing Web pages in Part VI, "Creating a Web Page with FrontPage Express."

Using the Explorer Bar

The Explorer Bar is a new feature of Internet Explorer. You can perform four different functions with the Explorer Bar. But you can only use one at a time. With the Explorer Bar, you can search the Internet, view your list of favorite Web sites, access channels that you have subscribed to, and look at your history list to see which Web sites you have visited recently.

1. **Click** on **View**. The View menu will appear.

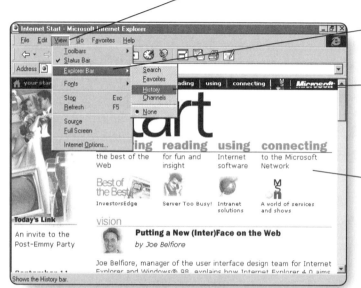

2. **Click** on **Explorer Bar**. A cascading menu will appear.

3. **Click** on **History**. The History list will appear in the Explorer Bar (located on the left side of the browser window).

4. **Click** on a **history item**. Internet Explorer will retrieve the page and display it in the right side of the browser window.

Changing Font Size

You can change the size of the text that displays on the Web pages you view.

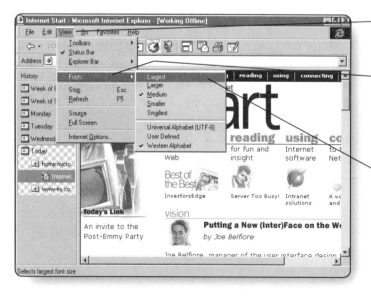

1. **Click** on **View**. The View menu will appear.

2. **Click** on **Fonts**. A cascading menu will appear. The size that Internet Explorer displays text will be checked in the menu list.

3. **Click** on a **font size**. The size that text displays at in the browser window will change.

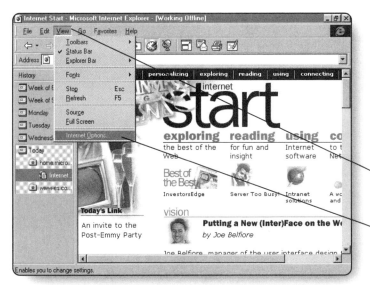

Changing Browser Options

You may want to change how you work with Internet Explorer. You can do this from one convenient place.

1. **Click** on **View**. The View menu will appear.

2. **Click** on **Internet Options**. The Options dialog box will open.

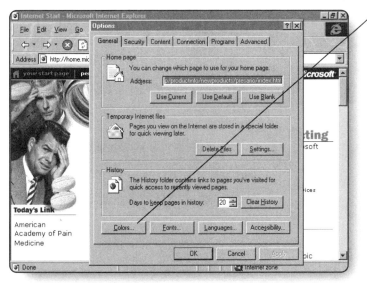

3. **Click** on **Colors**. The Colors dialog box will open.

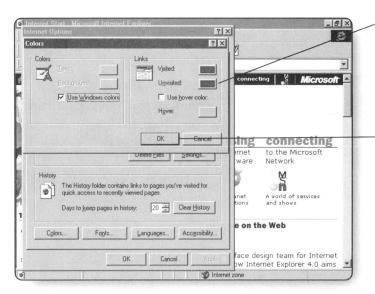

4. **Click** on the **Color buttons**. A color palette will appear and you can select a different color to display links on the Web pages you visit.

5. **Click** on **OK**. Your new link color preferences will be applied.

6. **Click** on the **Connection tab**. The Connection tab will come to the top of the stack.

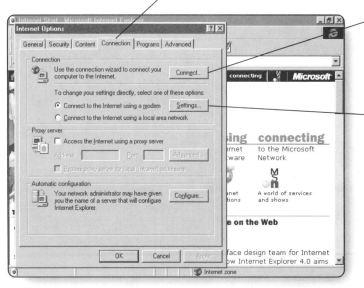

7. **Click** on **Connect**. The Internet Connection Wizard will start and you can configure a new dial-up connection.

8. **Click** on **Settings**. The Dial-up Settings dialog box will open and you can change the settings for an existing dial-up connection.

9. **Click** on the **Programs tab**. The Programs tab will come to the top of the stack.

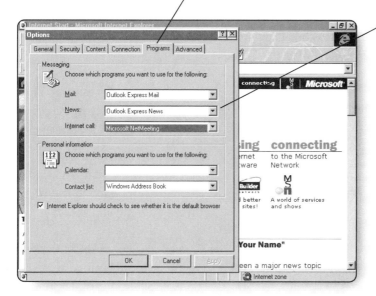

10. **Select** the **programs** in the Messaging area that Internet Explorer should start when you want to do things such as send e-mail or browse newsgroups.

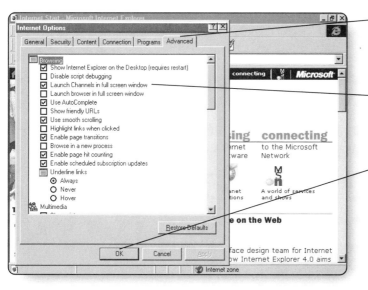

11. **Click** on the **Advanced tab**. The Advanced tab will come to the top of the stack.

12. **Click** on the **items** that you want enabled. A ✔ will appear next to those items you selected.

13. **Click** on **OK**. Your new settings will be applied.

STARTING YOUR ADVENTURE FROM THE ADDRESS BOX

The Address box is where you enter URL's for Web pages that you want to visit.

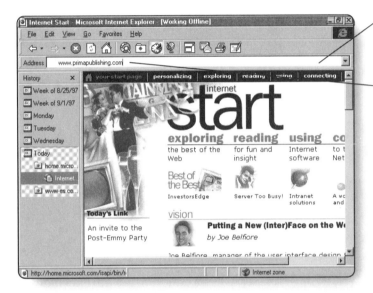

1. **Click** in the **Address box**. The URL that is currently in the Address box will be selected.

2. **Type** the **URL** of the Web page you want to visit. The first URL will disappear and the URL you are typing will display.

3. **Press** the **Enter key** when you are finished typing the URL. The Web page will appear in the browser window.

NOTE

If you have previously typed a URL into the Address box, Internet Explorer remembers the URL and will finish typing the URL for you. If it is the correct URL, press Enter and the requested page will display. If it is not the correct URL, continue typing the URL you want.

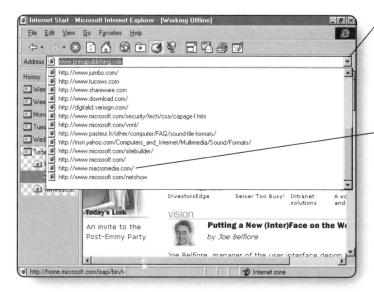

4. **Click** on the **down arrow** (▼) next to the Address list box. A list of URLs that you previously typed into the Address box will appear.

5. **Click** on a **URL**. The associated Web page will appear.

EXPLORING THE BROWSER WINDOW

The browser window is where you will be doing most of your work in Internet Explorer. Take a few minutes to learn your way around the screen.

1. **Click** on a **text hyperlink**. The associated Web page will appear in the browser window.

2. **Click** on a **graphical hyperlink**. The associated Web page will appear in the browser window.

3. Click on a **button** in a navigation bar. The associated Web page will appear in the browser window.

4. Click inside the **scroll bar**. The browser will scroll through the Web page you are viewing.

5 Checking Out Your Surf Gear

Now it's time to get Internet Explorer, and you, all set up for World Wide Web traveling. You'll want to keep track of the places you go to and the things that you bring back, as well as find out about how to keep things secure during your travels. In this chapter, you'll learn how to:

✦ Find or customize a Start page

✦ Track your Internet travels using the History and the Temporary Internet Files

✦ Keep your computer safe

GETTING YOUR START PAGE UP

You can customize your Start page to give you fingertip access to topics that interest you. You can select the providers that you want for each topic and have the information pipelined right to your desktop.

Building a Custom Start Page

The steps in the following section will lead you through customizing your own start page.

1. **Start Internet Explorer**. The browser will open and a start page will appear.

2. Type **home.microsoft.com/default.asp** and **press** the **Enter key** if you don't see the same start page. The Microsoft Internet Start Web page will appear.

3. **Click** on the **Personalizing link**. The Microsoft Start Personalizing Your Start Page Web page will appear.

4. **Click** on a **topic** under step 1. The topic will be selected.

5. **Click** on those **providers** under step 2 that you want included in your start page. A ✔ will appear in the box(es).

6. **Click** on **Next** under step 3. The next topic in the list under step 1 will appear.

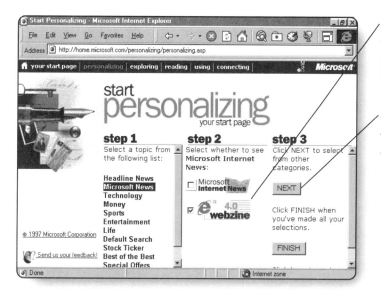

7. **Click** on those **providers** that you want included in your start page. A ✔ will appear in the box(es).

8. **Click** on **Next**. The next topic will appear. Continue through the list of topics.

9. Click on **providers** that you want included in your start page when you get to the last topic in the list. A ✔ will appear in the box next to those you selected.

10. Click on **Finish**. Your personalized start page will be created and will appear in the browser window.

11. Scroll through your personalized start page. You will notice the changes that were made.

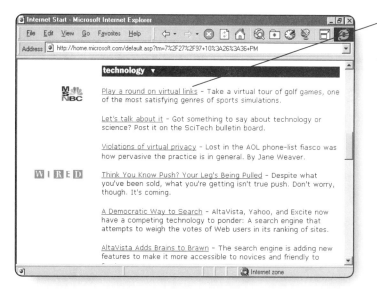

12. **Click** on a **hyperlink** to read a featured article. The hyperlink will be selected.

13. **Click** on a **topic heading**. The Start Personalizing Your Start Page Web page will appear.

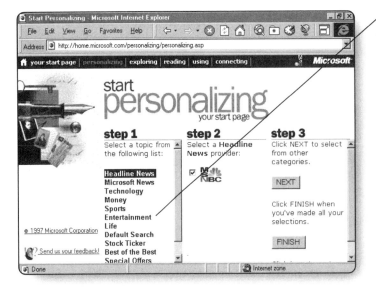

14. **Click** on the **topic** that you want to change in your start page. The list of providers for that topic will appear.

15. **Click** on **providers** to add or remove them. The ✔ will appear or disappear.

16. **Click** on **Finish**. Your changes will appear in the start page.

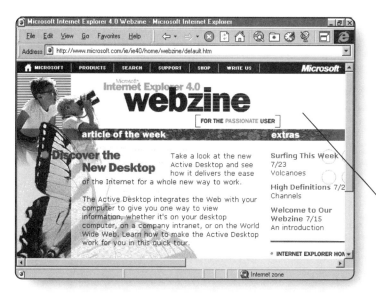

Choosing Your Own Start Page

You may choose any start page that you want. In fact you can make up different ones and switch them whenever you want.

1. Open the **page** that you want to use as a start page in the browser window.

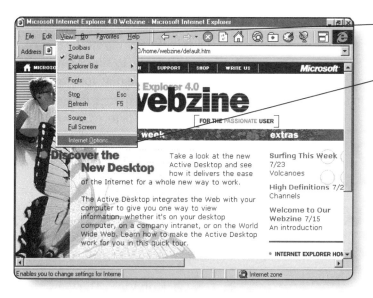

2. Click on **View**. The View menu will appear.

3. Click on **Internet Options**. The Internet Options dialog box will open.

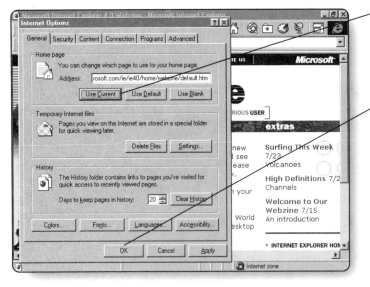

4. **Click** on the **Use Current button**. The URL for the page will appear in the Address: text box.

5. **Click** on **OK**. The next time that you open Internet Explorer, this page will appear in the browser window.

TRACKING YOUR WEB TRAVELS

Knowing where you have been helps in planning your next journey, making it easier for you to go directly to sites of interest or importance to you and avoid some of those that you don't need to see twice. The two tools in Internet Explorer for handling this are the History List and the Temporary Internet Files.

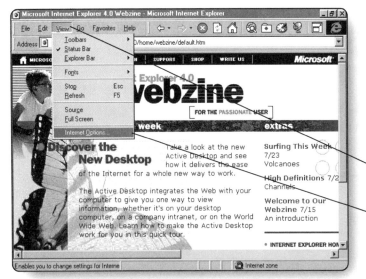

Using the History List

Use the History list to keep track of places you have been.

1. **Click** on **View**. The View menu will appear.

2. **Click** on **Internet Options**. The Internet Options dialog box will open.

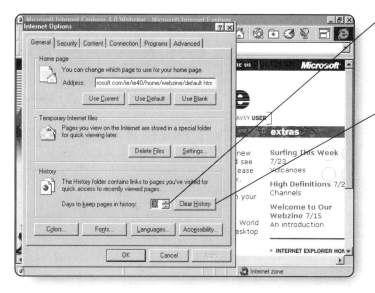

3. Click on the **up or down arrows** (◆) . The number of days that Web pages are stored in the history file will change.

4. Click on the **Clear History button**. A dialog box will open.

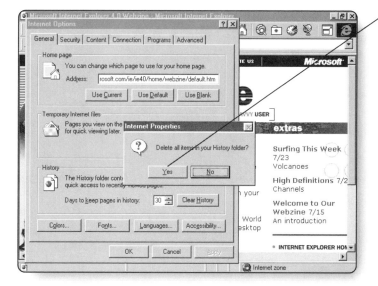

5. Click on **Yes**. The Web pages stored in the history file will be deleted from your computer.

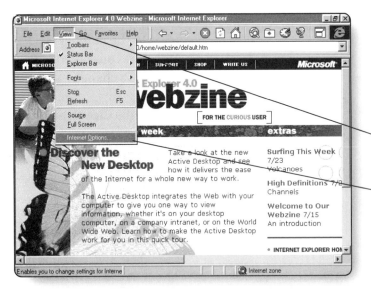

Using Temporary Internet Files

The Temporary Internet files will help you track your Web travels.

1. **Click** on **View**. The View menu will appear.

2. **Click** on **Internet Options**. The Internet Options dialog box will open.

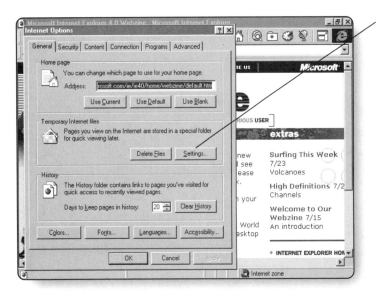

3. **Click** on the **Settings button**. The Settings dialog box will open.

4. **Click** on the **option button** corresponding to when you want Internet Explorer to check for an updated Web page before it displays the page stored on your computer. The option will be selected.

5. **Press** and **hold** the **mouse button** on the slider bar and **drag** to increase or decrease the amount of hard drive space that is used to store temporary Internet files.

6. **Release** the **mouse button**. The amount of hard drive space will be selected.

7. **Click** on the **View Files button**. The Temporary Internet Files folder will appear in a Windows Explorer window.

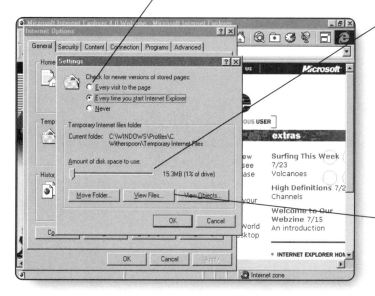

8. **Scroll** to view the contents of the folder.

9. **Click** on **Close**. The window will disappear.

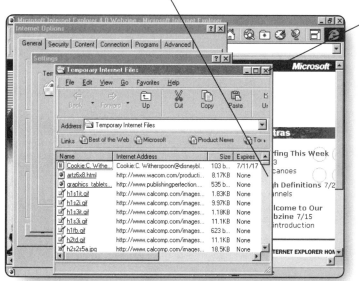

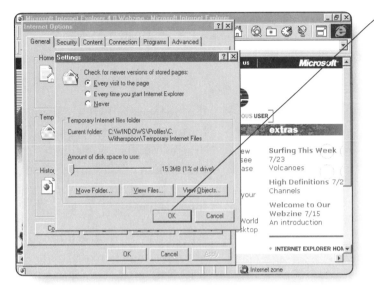

10. **Click** on **OK**. The Options dialog box will open.

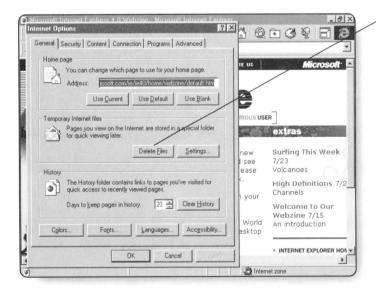

11. **Click** on the **Delete Files button**. A dialog box will open.

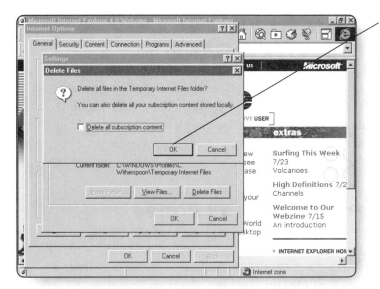

12. **Click** on **OK**. The files in the Temporary Internet Files folder will be deleted.

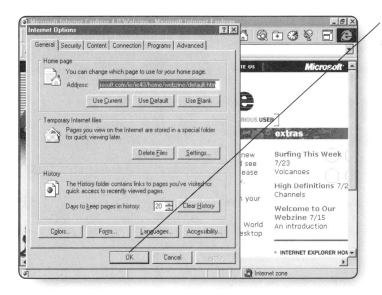

13. **Click** on **OK**. Your new settings will be applied.

KEEPING YOUR COMPUTER SAFE

We all would like to be free of viruses and other hazards, and we can do some things to help keep our documents and equipment safe. Internet Explorer has some tools for helping with security and setting up your computer for safe operation on the Web.

Setting Security Zones

Security zones allow you to set filters to keep some sites from downloading harmful content to your computer. The following shows you how to set the security zones options.

1. **Click** on **View**. The View menu will appear.

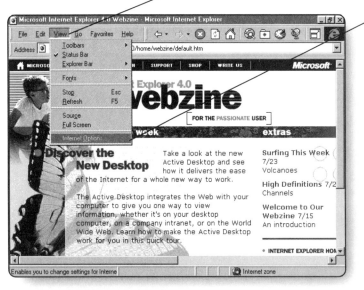

2. **Click** on **Internet Options**. The Options dialog box will open.

3. **Click** on the **Security tab**. The Security tab will come to the top of the stack.

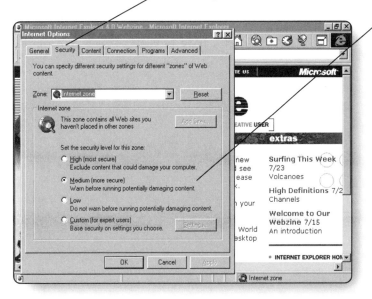

4. **Click** on the **option button** that corresponds to the security level you would like to use for your general Internet purposes. The option will be selected.

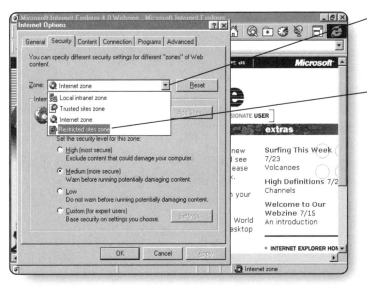

5. **Click** on the **down arrow (▼)** in the Zone: list box. A list of other security zones will appear.

6. **Click** on **Restricted sites zone**. This zone will appear in the Zone: text box.

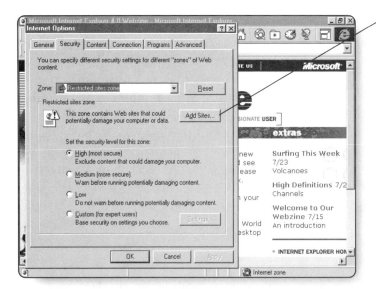

7. Click on the **Add Sites button**. The Restricted Sites Zone dialog box will open.

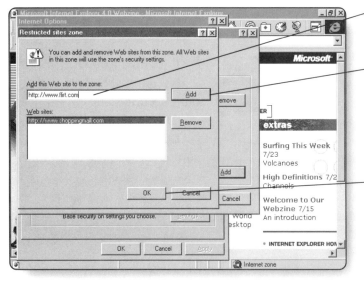

8. Type the **URL address** for the Web site.

9. Click on **Add**. This Web site will be added to the list of sites that will not be allowed to download content that could damage your computer.

10. Click on **OK**. The Security Options dialog box will open.

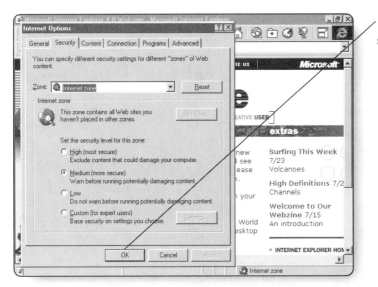

11. Click on **OK**. Your new settings will be applied.

Setting Content Ratings

Content ratings are a very handy way to keep track of the kind of things that may be contained on a Web site. You can set a password and allow the Content ratings system to filter out and deny access to sites that have unwanted content.

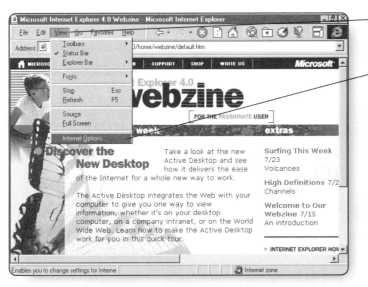

1. Click on **View**. The View menu will appear.

2. Click on **Internet Options**. The Internet Options dialog box will open.

3. **Click** on the **Content tab**. The Content tab will come to the top of the stack.

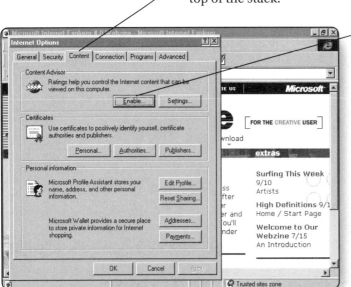

4. **Click** on the **Enable button**. The Create Supervisor Password dialog box will open.

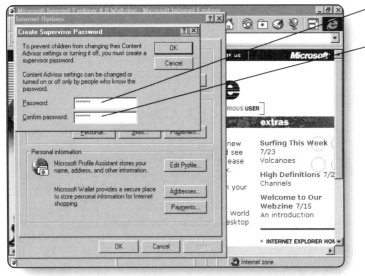

5. Type a **password**.

6. Type the **same password** a second time. This will confirm that you correctly typed the supervisor password.

NOTE

If you forget your supervisor password, you will not be able to turn the Content Advisor on and off, nor will you be able to change the ratings levels.

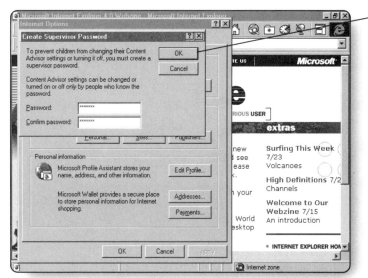

7. Click on **OK**. Your supervisor password and your ability to have sole access to the Content Advisor will be created and the Content Advisor dialog box will open.

8. Click on a **rating category**. Details about the rating category will appear in the lower part of the dialog box.

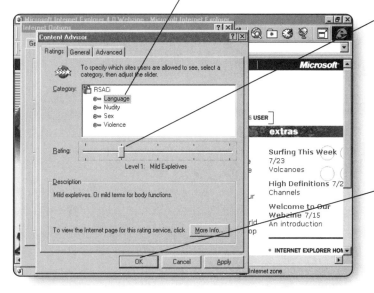

9. Press and hold the mouse button on the slider bar and drag until you find the desired tolerance level for the category.

10. Release the mouse button. The tolerance level will be selected.

11. Click on **OK**. The Content Options dialog box will open.

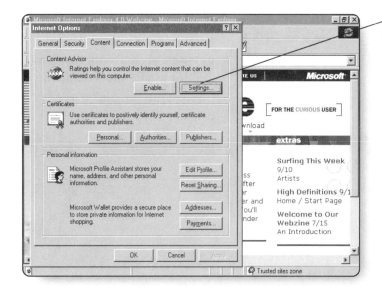

12. **Click** on the **Setting button**. The Supervisor Password Required dialog box will open.

13. **Type** your **supervisor password**.

14. **Click** on **OK**. The Content Advisor dialog box will open.

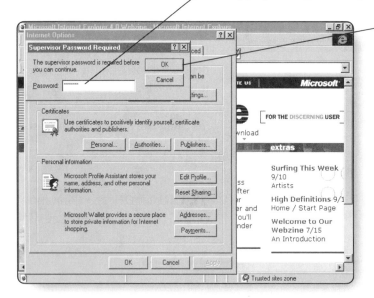

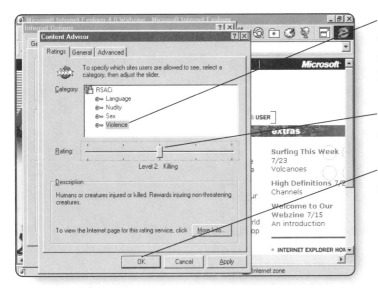

15. Click on the **category** for which you want to change the tolerance level. The category will be selected.

16. Use the **slider bar** again to change the tolerance level.

17. Click on **OK**. The Content Options dialog box will open.

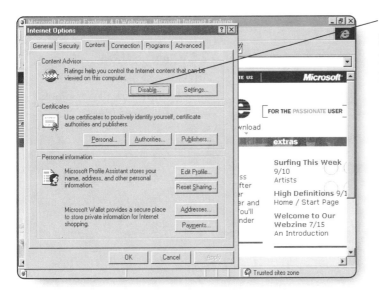

18. Click on the **Disable button**. The Supervisor Password Required dialog box will open.

19. Type your **supervisor password**.

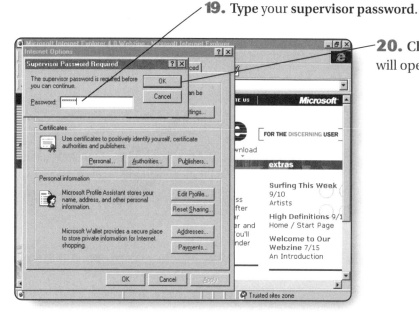

20. Click on **OK**. A dialog box will open.

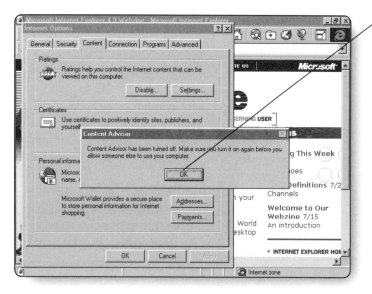

21. Click on **OK**. The Content Advisor will be disabled and your computer will not block access to rated sites.

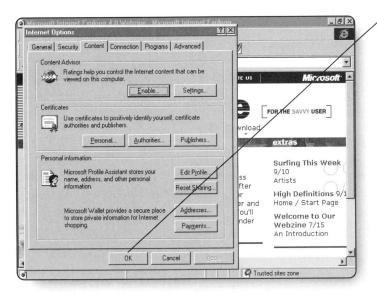

22. Click on **OK**. The Content Advisor settings will be applied.

Securing the Cookie Jar

Cookies are small files that contain information about your visits to a Web site. Every time you visit a Web site, the site's server looks for this file so that you may continue browsing the site from the place where you concluded your previous visit.

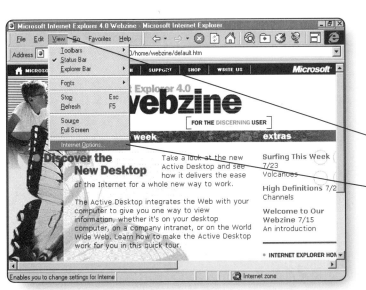

You can decide what to do about cookies that ask to be downloaded to your computer. You may make the decision for each cookie if you want or you can elect to have all or none.

1. Click on **View**. The View menu will appear.

2. Click on **Internet Options**. The Internet Options dialog box will open.

3. **Click** on the **Advanced tab**. The Advanced tab will come to the top of the stack.

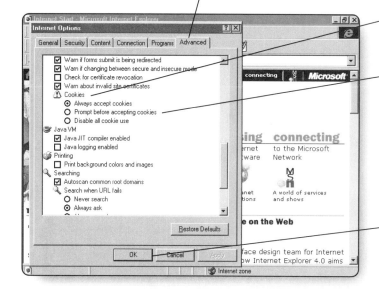

4. **Scroll down** the list until you find the Cookies category.

5. **Click** on the **option button** to prompt you when a cookie wants to be downloaded to your computer. The option will be selected, and you will have to make the decision to accept a cookie or not.

6. **Click** on **OK**. The cookie settings will be applied.

6 Working with Favorites

Internet Explorer provides you with a way to keep a list of those Web pages that you want to visit on a regular basis or just want to save for future reference. This is done through a feature called "Favorites." By using the Favorites feature, you can keep a list of Web pages organized in one convenient place. You can do more than just keep one long list of URL addresses. You can organize Favorites into folders to list Web pages by topic categories. This makes it easier to find the Web page you need. You can also subscribe to Favorite Web pages. When you subscribe to a Web site, Internet Explorer lets you know when there has been a change made to that page. In this chapter, you'll learn how to:

✦ Add a Web site to your list of Favorites

✦ Organize your Favorites so they are easy to find

✦ Set subscriptions to Web pages

ADDING A SITE TO YOUR LIST OF FAVORITES

As you surf the Internet, you will come across thousands and thousands of Web sites. When you find a Web site that you think you'll want to visit again later, you'll need to make a note of its URL address. You could always write the URL address for the Web site on a piece of paper. An easier way to keep a list of Web sites is to let Internet Explorer do this for you.

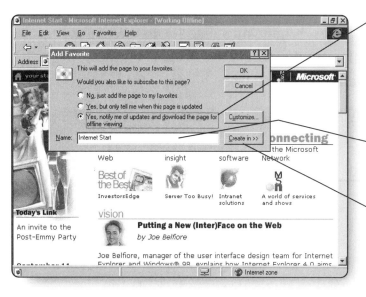

1. Go to the **page** you want to add to your collection of favorite pages.

2. Click on **Favorites**. The Favorites menu will appear.

3. Click on **Add to Favorites**. The Add Favorite dialog box will open.

4. Click on the **Yes, notify me of updates and download the page for offline viewing**. Internet Explorer will download the Web page to your computer so that you can view it while offline.

5. Leave the **default name** for the page in the Name: text box or type a different name.

6. Click on the **Create in button**. This will expand the dialog box to show the available folders where you can store your favorite.

7. Select a **folder** in which to add the favorite. The folder will be selected.

8. Click on **OK**. The page will be added to your list of favorites.

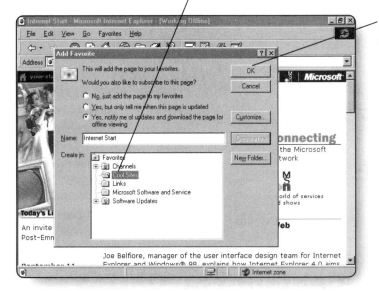

VIEWING A FAVORITE PAGE

1. Click on **Favorites**. The Favorites menu will appear.

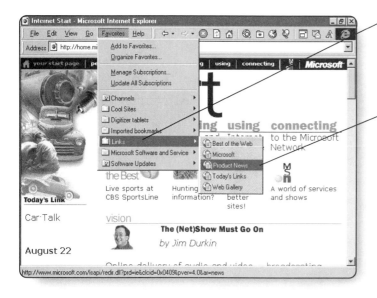

2. **Move** your **mouse pointer** down to the folder in which the favorite is located. A cascading menu will appear.

3. **Click** on the **favorite** that you want to open. The page will appear in the browser window.

ORGANIZING FAVORITES

After you've created your list of favorites, you may find that the list has become cumbersome to work with. You can make favorites easier to work with by grouping favorites into folders by categories. You may want to move a favorite from one folder to another folder if you're having a hard time remembering where you put it.

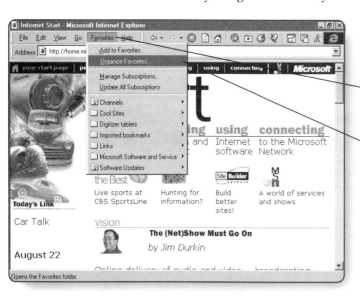

1. **Click** on **Favorites**. The Favorites menu will appear.

2. **Click** on **Organize Favorites**. The Organize Favorites dialog box will open.

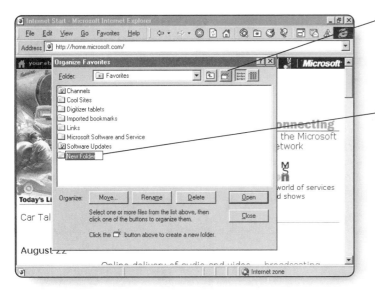

3. **Click** on the **Create New Folder button**. A new folder icon will appear in the Folder: window.

4. **Type** a **name** for the new folder.

5. **Press** the **Enter key**. The new folder will be created.

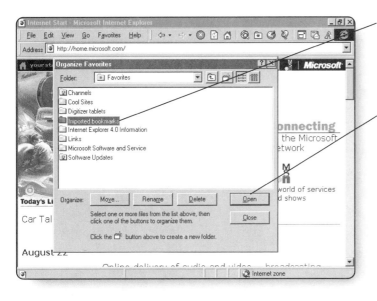

6. **Click** on the **folder** that contains the favorite listing you want to move. The folder will selected.

7. **Click** on **Open**. The folder will open and display the list of favorites contained in it.

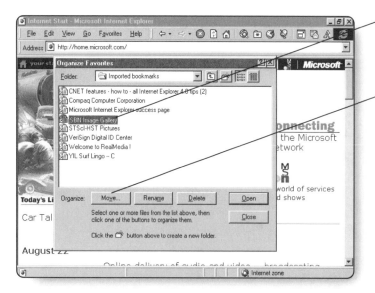

8. **Click** on the **favorite** that you want to move. The favorite will be selected.

9. **Click** on the **Move button**. The Browse for Folder dialog box will open.

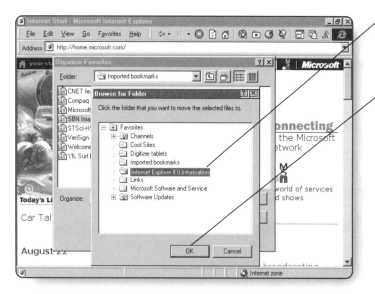

10. **Click** on the **folder** that you just created. The folder will be selected.

11. **Click** on **OK**. The favorite will be moved to the new folder, and the Browse for Folder dialog box will close.

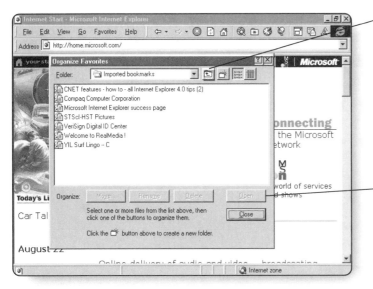

12. **Click** on the **Up One Level button**. The top level of the Favorites folder will appear.

13. **Click** on the **folder** that contains the favorite you just moved. The folder will be selected.

14. **Click** on **Open**. The folder will open and the favorite you just moved will appear.

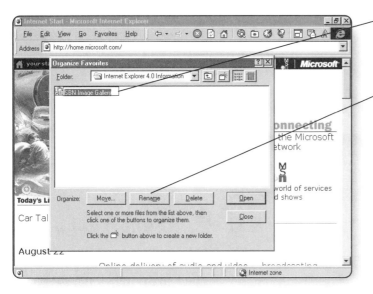

15. **Click** on the **favorite** you just moved. The favorite will be selected.

16. **Click** on the **Rename button**. A box will appear around the name of the favorite.

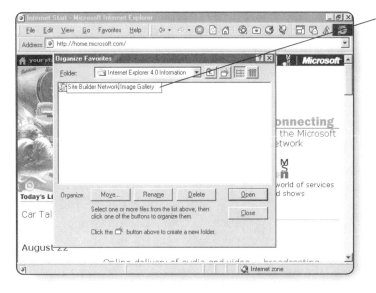

17. Type a **new name** for the favorite.

18. Press the **Enter key**. The favorite will be renamed.

SUBSCRIBING TO A WEB SITE

Most Web pages change from time to time. Some Web pages may contain magazine-type articles that change at regular intervals. Some Web pages may only make changes occasionally. It could take a lot of time to go to each Web page and see if the page has changed. To save yourself some time, let Internet Explorer keep track of when Web sites change. Internet Explorer will also notify you when changes are made.

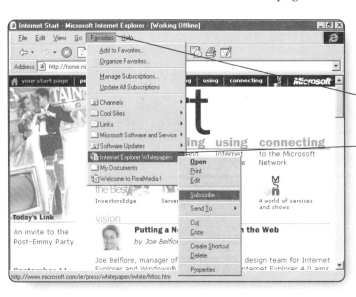

1. **Click** on **Favorites**. The Favorites menu will appear.

2. Move your **mouse pointer** down to the folder that contains the favorite to which you want to subscribe. A cascading menu will appear.

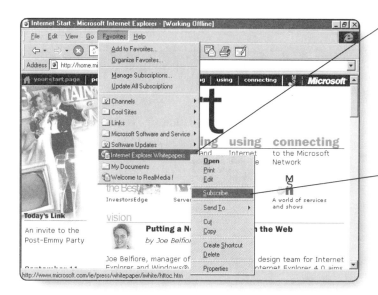

3. Move your **mouse pointer** to the favorite to which you want to subscribe. The favorite will be highlighted.

4. **Right-click** on the **favorite**. A shortcut menu will open.

5. **Click** on **Subscribe**. The Subscribe Favorite dialog box will open.

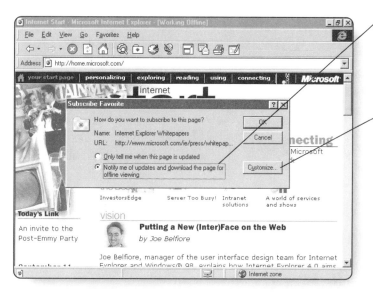

6. **Click** on the **Notify me of updates and download the page for offline viewing option**. The option will be selected.

7. **Click** on the **Customize button**. The Web Site Subscription Wizard will open.

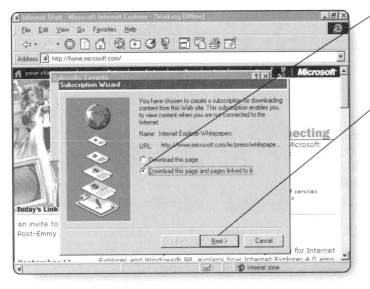

8. **Click** on the **Download this page and pages linked to it option**. The option will be selected.

9. **Click** on **Next**. The next step of the wizard will appear.

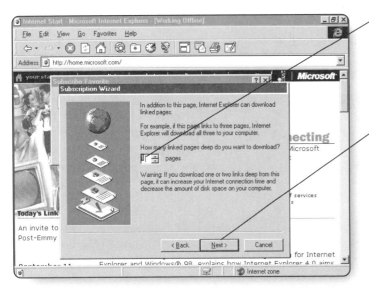

10. **Type** the **maximum number** of hyperlinked pages that you want to download along with the page to which you subscribed.

11. **Click** on **Next**. The next screen of the wizard will appear.

12. Click on the **Yes, send an e-mail message to the following address: option button**. The option will be selected.

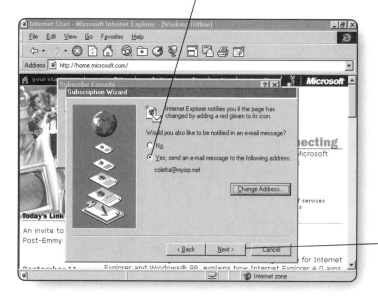

13. Click on **Next**. The next screen of the wizard will appear.

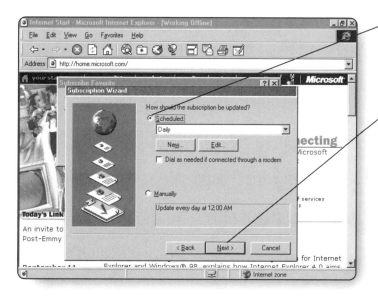

14. Click on the **option button** that corresponds to the type of schedule you want to set. The option will be selected.

15. Click on **Next**. The next screen in the wizard will appear.

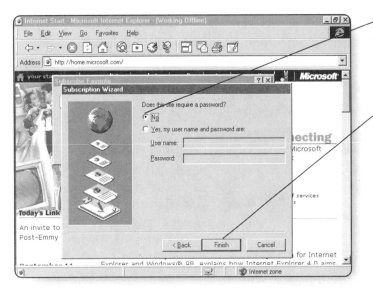

16. **Click** on an **option button** to specify whether or not you need a password to access the site. The option will be selected.

17. **Click** on **Finish**. The Subscribe Favorite dialog box will open.

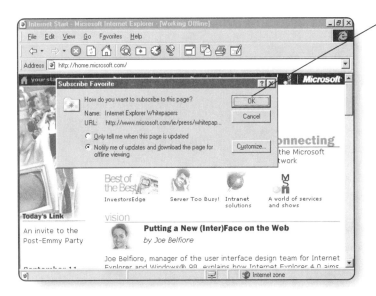

18. **Click** on **OK**. The subscription settings will be applied.

CHANGING SUBSCRIPTION SCHEDULES

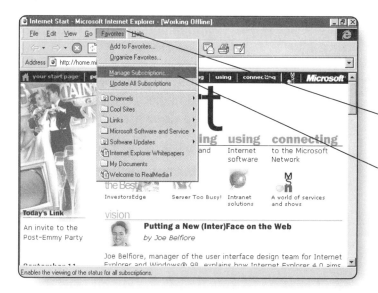

You may decide that you want to change the schedule that a particular Web site uses to check for updated content.

1. **Click** on **Favorites**. The Favorites menu will appear.

2. **Click** on **Manage Subscriptions**. The Subscription window will open.

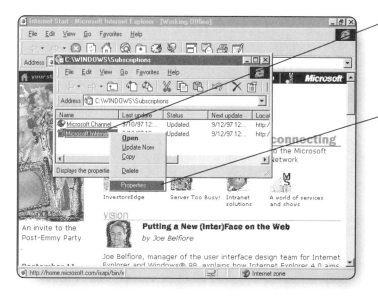

3. **Right-click** on the **name** of the subscription to which you want to make changes. A shortcut menu will appear.

4. **Click** on **Properties**. The Properties dialog box will open.

5. **Click** on the **Schedule tab**. The tab will come to the top of the stack.

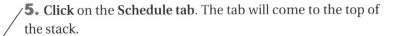

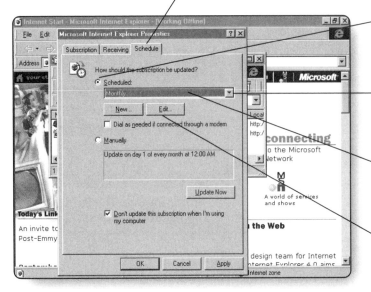

6. **Click** on the **Scheduled option button**. The option will be selected.

7. **Click** on the **down arrow** (▼) next to the Scheduled: list box. A drop-down list will appear.

8. **Click** on the **frequency** of checking for updated pages. The frequency will be selected.

9. **Click** on **Edit**. The Custom Schedule dialog box will open.

10. **Click** on an **option button** to select the type of schedule to set. The option will be selected.

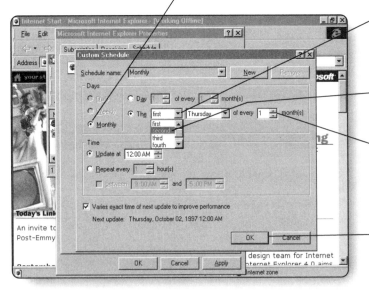

11. **Click** on the **down arrow** (▼) in the selected option. A drop-down list will appear.

12. **Click** on a **frequency**. The frequency will be selected.

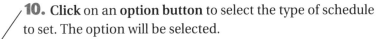

13. **Click** on the **up and down arrows** (♦) to change the time that Internet Explorer will check the Web page for changes.

14. **Click** on **OK**. The Properties dialog box will open.

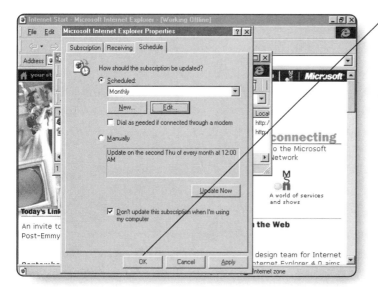

15. **Click** on **OK**. The Properties dialog box will close, the update schedule for the page will be updated, and the Subscription window will appear.

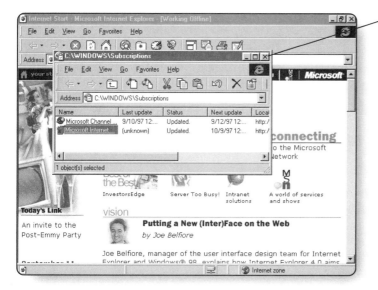

16. **Click** on the **Close button** (⊠). The Subscription window will close.

TIP

You don't always have to wait for Internet Explorer to check for updated content on the sites to which you are subscribed. To manually update your subscriptions, select the Update All Subscriptions command from the Favorites menu.

7 Surfing on the Web

The Web contains worlds of information and exciting new things, and Internet Explorer can bring all of them to you. It can even help you find the things that you want and display them for you, or help you bring them back to your computer. In this chapter, you'll learn how to:

✦ Use the Search tools

✦ Watch a NetShow movie

✦ Download and save files

✦ View and participate in multimedia

SEARCHING THE WEB

The search facilities available with Internet Explorer can help you find things that you want easily and effortlessly. This section will take you step-by-step through the process of using the search engines to find whatever you might be looking for.

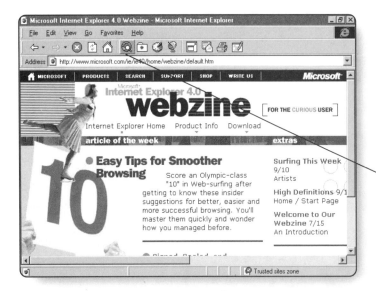

Searching for Web Pages

The following screens and steps will lead you through utilizing a search engine to find information or items of interest.

1. **Click** on the **Search button**. The Search Bar will appear.

NOTE

The search engine that displays when the Search Bar is opened changes every day. In case you don't like the default search engine, you will learn how to select a different search engine later in this section.

2. **Click** in the **search text box** and **type** a **few words** to describe what you are looking for.

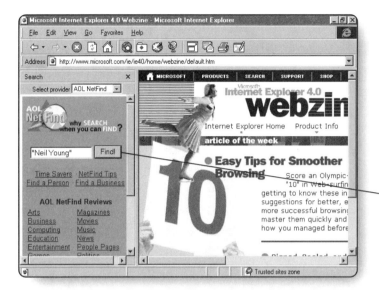

3. **Click** on the **Find button**. The search engine will compile a list of Web pages that match your search terms.

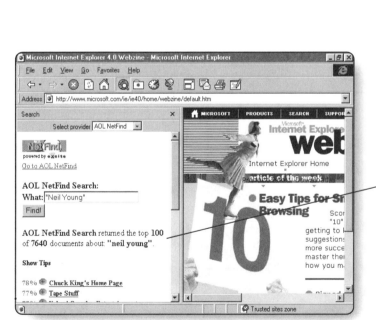

4. **Scroll through** the list of search results.

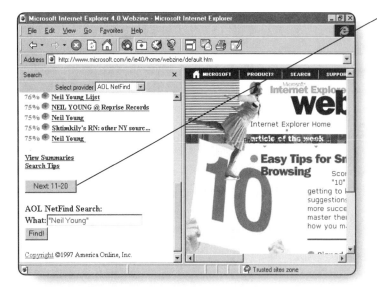

5. **Click** on **Next**. The next group of search results will appear in the Search Bar.

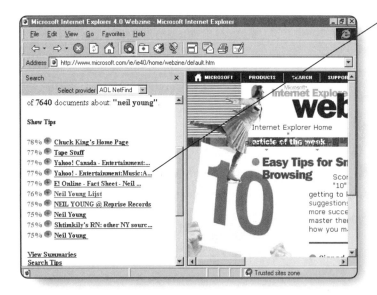

6. **Click** on a **search result hyperlink**. The linked Web page will appear on the right side of the browser window.

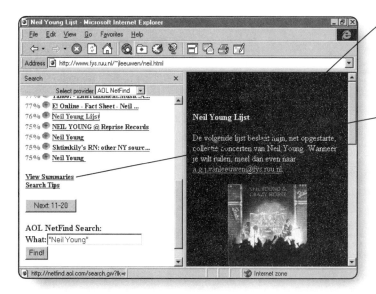

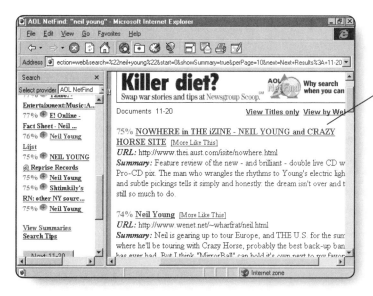

7. Look through the **Web page** to see whether it contains the information that you are looking for.

8. Click on **View Summaries**. A brief description of what the Web page contains will appear.

NOTE

View Summaries may not be available on all search engines. If a View Summaries option is not available, place the mouse pointer over a hyperlink until a screen tip appears. The screen tip will display a summary of the Web page.

9. Click on a **search result hyperlink** that may meet your needs after checking the summary page's list of additional information about the search results. The associated Web page will appear on the right side of the browser window.

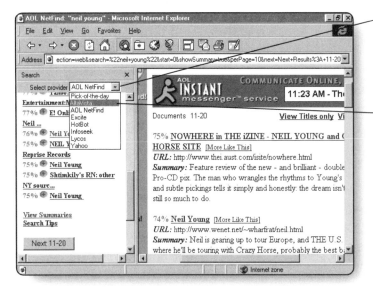

10. Click on the **down arrow** (▼) on the Select Provider drop-down list. A list of available search engines will appear.

11. Click on the **search engine** that you want to use. The search engine's search page will appear in the Search Bar.

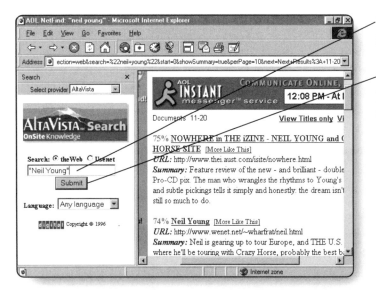

12. Type your **search query** in the text box.

13. Click on the **Submit button**. A list of search results will appear in the Search Bar.

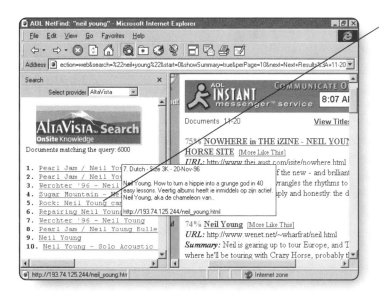

14. Place the **mouse pointer** over the hyperlink that you think you may want to view. A screen tip will appear showing detailed information about the search result. If you think that this search result contains the information you are looking for, click on its hyperlink.

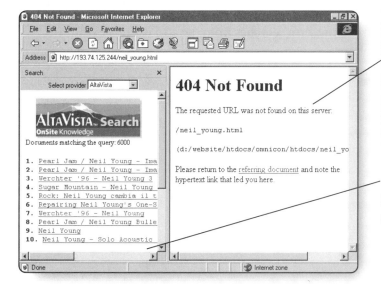

NOTE

Some search results can be outdated. When that happens, a page telling you that the URL address was not found will appear.

15. Click on the **Next hyperlink**. The next group of search results will appear.

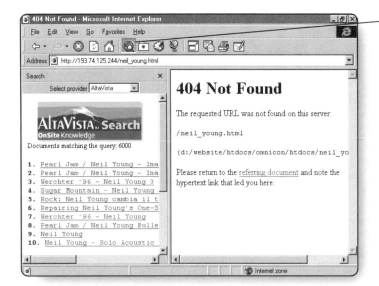

16. **Click** on the **Search button**. The Search Bar will close.

NOTE

When you close the Search Bar, your search results will be lost.

Searching from the Address Box

You can perform searches from the address box in Internet Explorer.

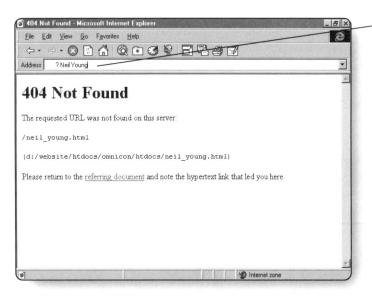

1. **Type** a **question mark** followed by your **search query** in the Address text box and **press** the **Enter key**. Internet Explorer will search Yahoo!'s database and return a list of search results.

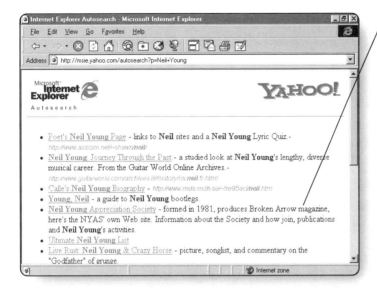

2. Click on a **hyperlink** that closely matches your search request.

Searching for People

Internet Explorer can help you find people on the Net by making access to directory services available to you from inside the browser.

1. Click on the **Start button**. The Start menu will appear.

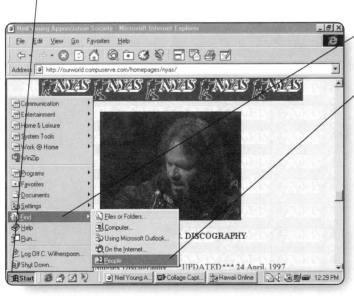

2. Click on **Find**. The Find menu will appear.

3. Click on **People**. The Find People dialog box will open.

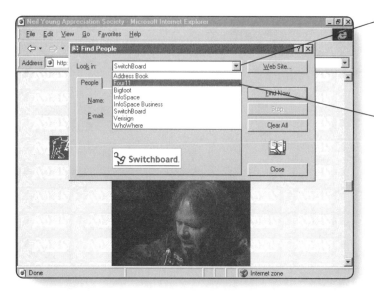

4. Click on the down arrow (▼) next to the Look in: list box. A list of available directory services will appear.

5. Click on the directory service that you want to use. The dialog box will change to show the criteria by which the directory service allows you to search.

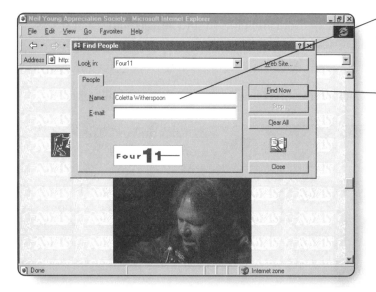

6. Type the name of the person you are looking for in the Name: text box.

7. Click on Find Now. The directory service looks for any matches to your search query.

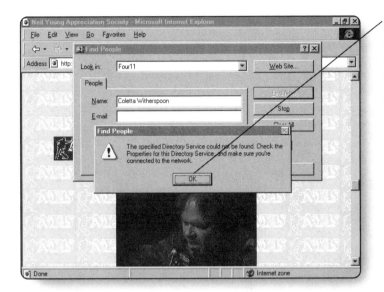

8. Click on **OK** if a dialog box has opened, letting you know that no matches were found. The Find People dialog box will open.

9. Click on a **different directory service**. The directory service will be selected.

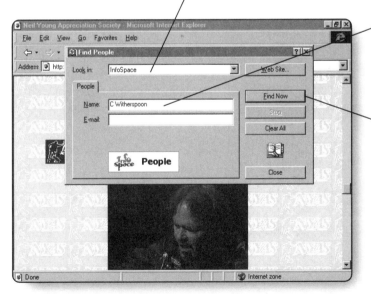

10. Type the **name** you are searching for to something slightly different to possibly return better search results.

11. Click on **Find Now**. A dialog box will open asking you to wait until the directory service finishes its search. When the directory service finishes it search, the search results will appear at the bottom of the Find People dialog box.

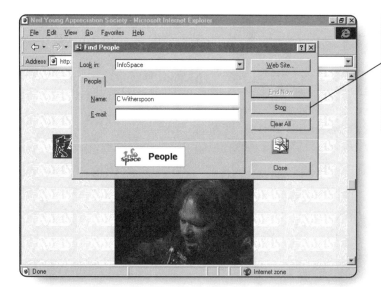

NOTE

Click on Stop if you don't want to wait while the directory service compiles the search results.

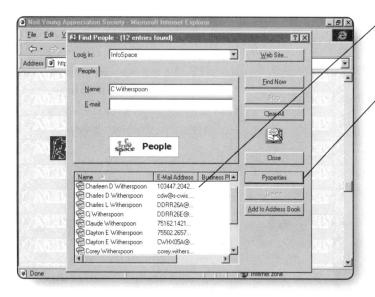

12. **Click** on the **name** of the person you were looking for. The name will be selected.

13. **Click** on **Properties**. The Properties dialog box for the person you were looking for will open.

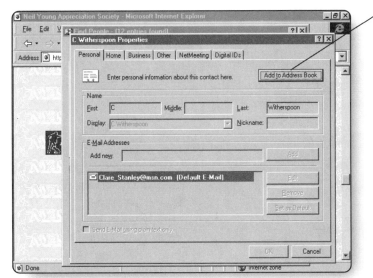

14. **Click** on **Add to Address
Book.** The person's e-mail
address will be added to your
Windows Address Book and
you will be able to send him
or her e-mail by using your
Address Book.

VIEWING MULTIMEDIA

Viewing multimedia is one of Explorer's strong suits. You can
play in a virtual world or watch a NetShow video, or you can
learn about Dynamic HTML. Internet Explorer does a
marvelous job of bringing it all to you.

Playing with VRML

VRML (Virtual Reality Markup Language) can be used to create
interactive 3-D worlds that you can move about inside with the
tools supplied with Internet Explorer. It is one of the more
exciting new technologies today. The people at the NASA Jet
Propulsion Laboratory have already used some of those
technologies to let millions of us here on Earth experience
traveling with the Sojourner Rover on Mars.

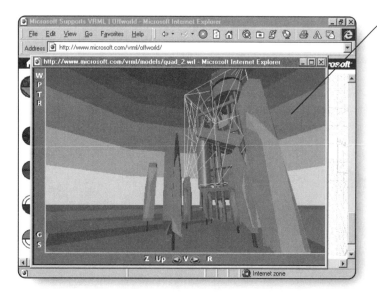

1. Open a **virtual world**. The virtual world may appear in the browser or it may appear in the VRML viewer.

NOTE

You can find a number of links to virtual worlds on Microsoft's Web site. Point your browser to http://www.microsoft.com /vrml for information about VRML and to http://www.microsoft.com /vrml/offworld for a list of VRML Web sites.

2. Click on the **Walk** button.

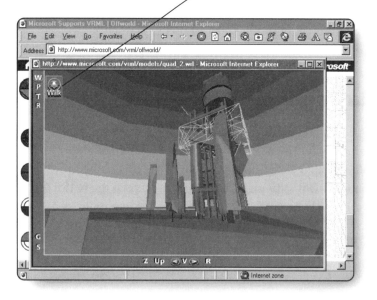

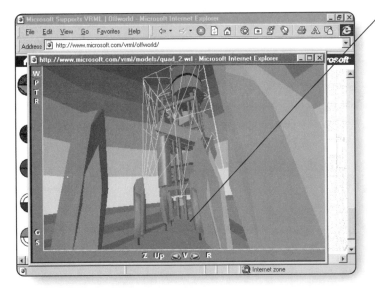

3. Press and hold the **mouse button** after moving the mouse pointer into the virtual world and **drag** the **mouse** toward the place in the virtual world that you want to see in more detail. The virtual world will come closer and you will be able to see more of the world's details.

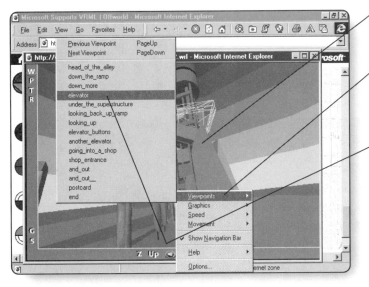

4. Right-click on the **virtual world**. A menu will appear.

5. Click on **Viewpoints**. A list of places in the virtual world will appear.

6. Click on a **place**. You will see the virtual world move in front of your eyes until the place you selected is in view.

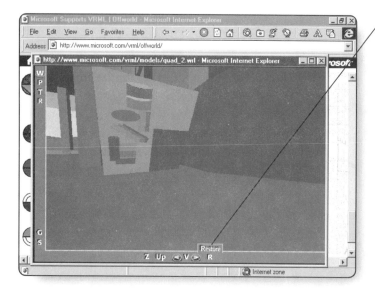

7. **Click** on the **Restore button**. The original view of the virtual world will appear.

Watching a NetShow Video

NetShow will enable you to download video to your computer from pages on the Web and view it while it is streaming in.

1. **Click** on a **NetShow link**. The NetShow window will appear.

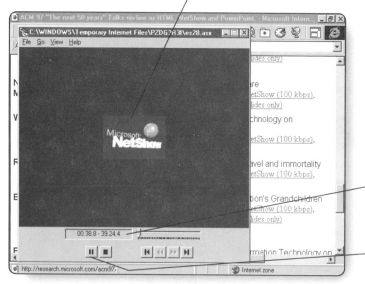

NOTE

You can find a list of NetShow sites from the Microsoft NetShow Web site (located at http://www. microsoft.com/netshow/ examples.htm).

2. **Watch** the **status bar** while the NetShow video begins to download.

3. When a portion of the video has downloaded, the video will automatically begin to play.

4. **Click** on **any** of the following buttons:

✦ Previous Track button. The NetShow video will start playing at the beginning of the previous section of the video.

✦ Rewind button. The NetShow video will return to the beginning of the video but will not begin playing automatically.

✦ Forward button. The NetShow video will advance toward the end of the video.

✦ Next Track button. The NetShow video will start playing at the beginning of the next section of the video.

5. **Click** on the **Stop button**. The video will stop at the place where it was being viewed.

WORKING WITH FILES

Working with files is an important part of the Internet Explorer's function. After all, the original reason for creating a computer network was the capacity to transfer files, and it still is the most popular use.

Downloading Files

Everyone finds something desirable to download from the Web. That something might be music, pictures, text, sound, video, or something containing all of those. Or you might want to download an application that you simply must have.

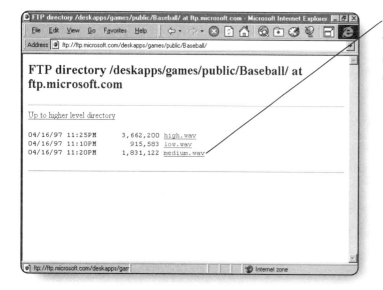

1. **Click** on the **file** that you want to download to your computer. The File Download dialog box will open.

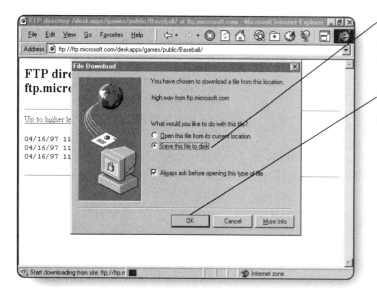

2. **Click** on the **option button** to save the file to disk. The option will be selected.

3. **Click** on **OK**. The Save As dialog box will open.

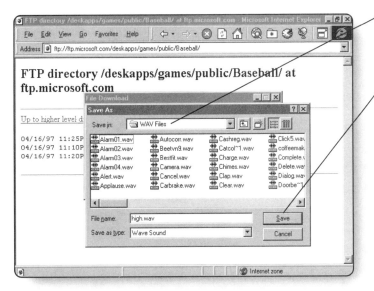

4. **Select** the **folder** where you want to store the file. The folder will be selected.

5. **Click** on **Save**. The file will begin to download to the folder that you specified on your computer.

Using a Right-Click to Save Files

Saving files after they are downloaded to your computer is as easy as performing a couple of mouse-clicks. Internet Explorer has a very nice way of letting you save things directly from the download so that they go to the place that they belong as they download.

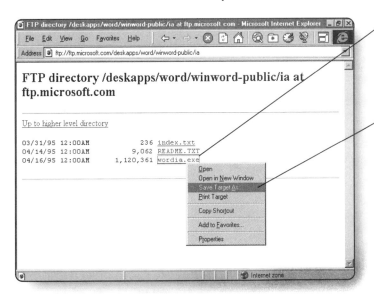

1. **Right-click** on the **file** that you want to download to your computer. A shortcut menu will appear.

2. **Click** on **Save Target As**. The file will begin downloading.

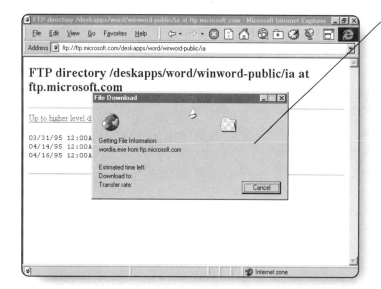

The File Download dialog box tells you that the file information is being accessed. After the file information is obtained, the Save As dialog box will open.

NOTE

If you decide that you really don't want to save that file, click on the Cancel button.

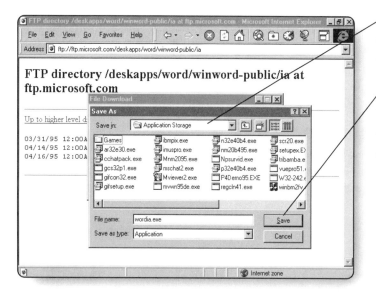

3. Select the folder in which you want to store the file. The folder will be selected.

4. Click on Save. The file will begin to download to the folder that you specified on your computer.

8 Putting Active Content on the Desktop

The Active Desktop is one of the fun things to come out of recent innovations in Internet technologies and it is an entertaining and informative tool that you can have right at your fingertips. Active content will help keep you informed and up-to-date on the subjects in which you have an interest, and will provide you with a nice window on the world through the Internet or an intranet. In this chapter, you'll learn how to:

✦ Add components to your desktop

✦ Subscribe to channels

PLACING COMPONENTS ON THE DESKTOP

Desktop components represent a new technology that creates interactive desktop shortcuts. These components come in varied sizes and can be HTML documents or images. Desktop components work like Web pages: when you click on a hyperlink contained in the component, you will access the linked Web page through the Internet Explorer browser. Desktop components can also be set up so that their content is updated on a regular schedule. This schedule can be customized so that you choose when the updates will occur and how.

1. Type **http://www.microsoft.com/ie/ie40/gallery/** in the Address text box to access the Microsoft Active Desktop Gallery.

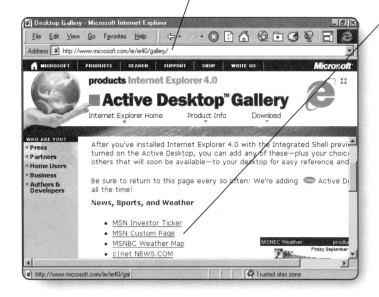

2. **Click** on the **desktop component** that you want to download. The download page for the desktop component will appear.

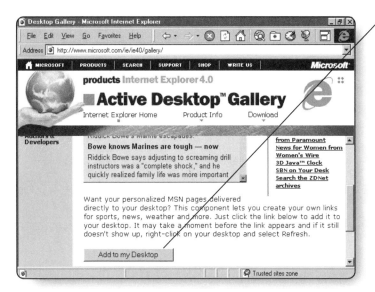

3. **Click** on the **Add to my Desktop button**. The component will begin to download and the Subscribe dialog box will open.

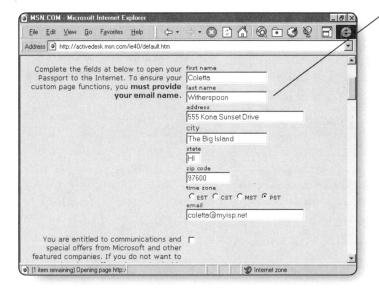

4. **Scroll down** the page to the Personal Information section and **type** as much **personal information** as you want to divulge in the text boxes.

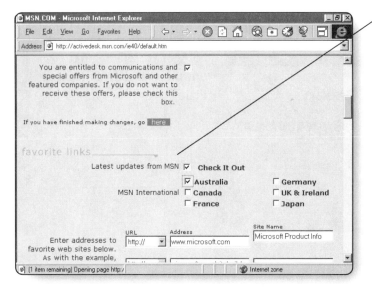

5. **Scroll down** to the **Favorite Links** section and **click** on **preselected links** that you want added to your custom page. A ✔ will appear in the boxes next to the links that you selected.

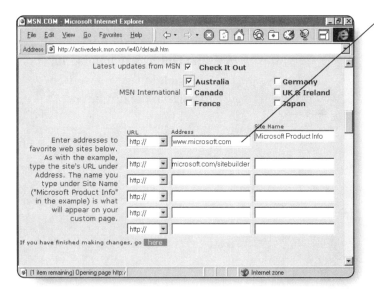

6. **Scroll down** to the end of the **Favorite Links** section and **type** the **URL addresses** for other Web pages that you want to add to the list.

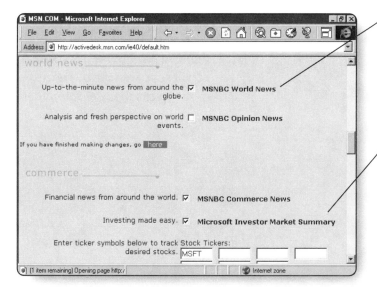

7. Scroll down to the World News section and click on the news services to which you want quick access. A ✔ will appear in the boxes next to the news services that you selected.

8. Click on the investment news services that you want in the Commerce section. A ✔ will appear in the boxes next to the services that you selected.

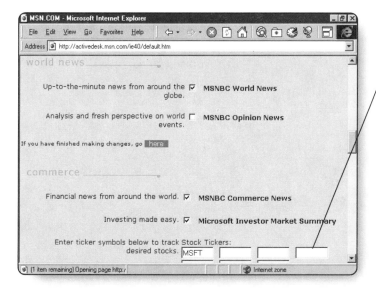

NOTE

You can also have a scrolling stock ticker display with a list of stocks in which you have an interest.

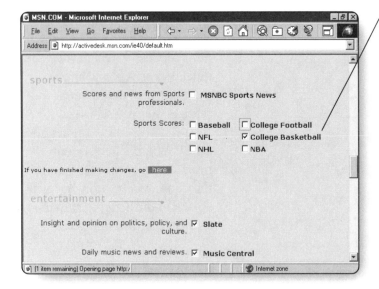

9. **Scroll down** to the **Sports section** and **click** on the **sports** that you want to keep track of. A ✔ will appear in the boxes next to the sports that you selected.

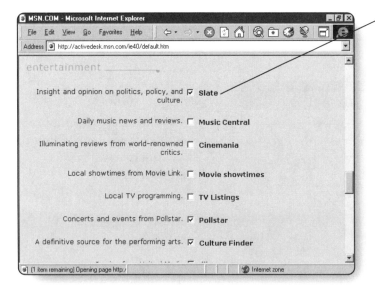

10. **Scroll down** to the **Entertainment section** and **click** on the **entertainment services** to which you want to have access. A ✔ will appear in the boxes next to the services that you selected.

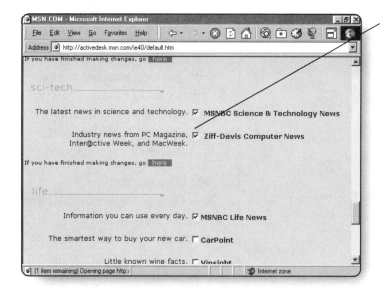

11. **Scroll down** to the **Sci-Tech** section and **click** on the **Technology magazines** that you want to add to your custom page. A ✔ will appear in the boxes next to the magazines that you selected.

12. **Scroll down** to the **Life** section and **click** on the **information services** in which you are interested. A ✔ will appear in the boxes next to the services that you selected.

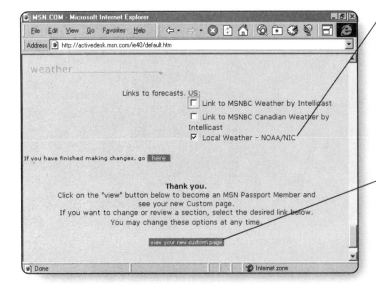

13. **Scroll down** to the **Weather** section and **click** on the **weather services** that you will need in order to make a decision about whether to take a raincoat with you when you go shopping. A ✔ will appear in the boxes next to the services that you selected.

14. **Click** on the **View Your New Custom Page button** when you are satisfied with your selections. The final page of the desktop component installation will appear.

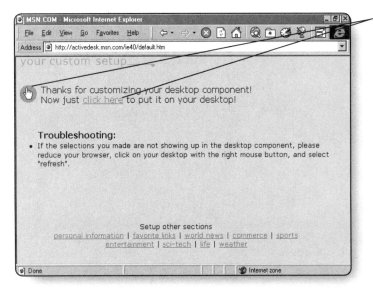

15. **Click** on the **Hand icon** or the **Click here hyperlink**. A Security Alert dialog box will appear.

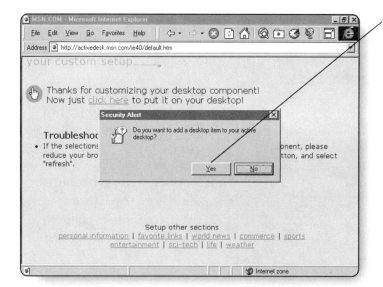

16. **Click** on **Yes**. The Add item to Active Desktop dialog box will appear.

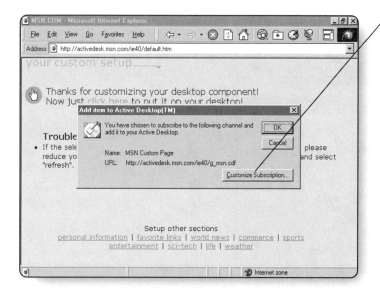

17. **Click** on **Customize Subscription**. The Subscription Wizard will appear.

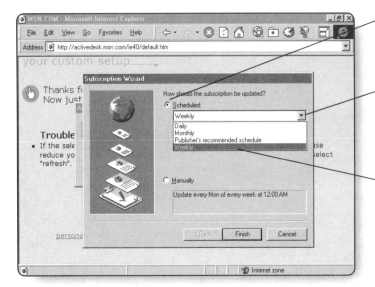

18. Click on the **Scheduled option**. The option will be selected.

19. Click the **down arrow** (▼) on the Scheduled drop-down list. A list of schedules will appear.

20. Click on the **schedule** you want to use to update the desktop component content. The schedule will be selected.

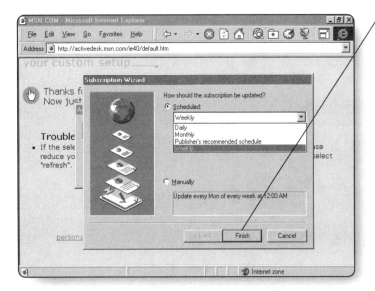

21. Click on **Finish**. The Add item to Active Desktop dialog box will appear.

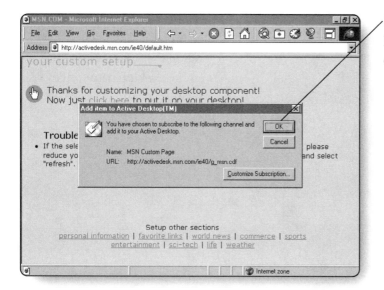

22. Click on **OK**. The Downloading Subscriptions dialog box will open.

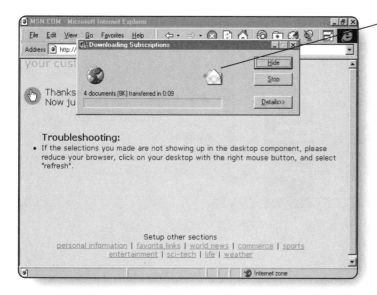

23. Wait while the **subscription content** downloads to your desktop. The browser window will appear when the download is complete.

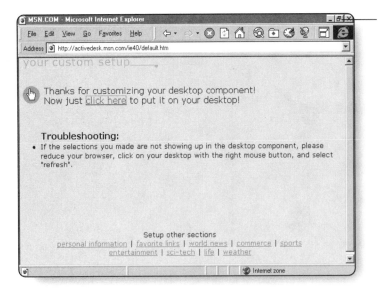

24. **Click** the **Minimize button**. The browser will become an icon on the Windows Taskbar and the desktop component will appear.

25. **Place** the **mouse pointer** over each of the blue squares at the top of the component. The name of the link will appear to the right.

26. **Click** on a **link**. The content for that category will appear.

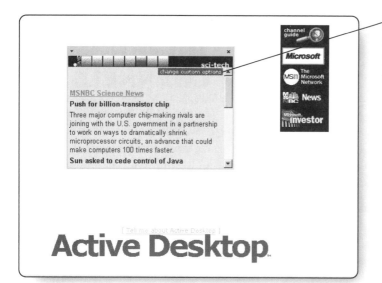

27. Click on the **Change Custom Options hyperlink**. The change Custom Options Web page will appear.

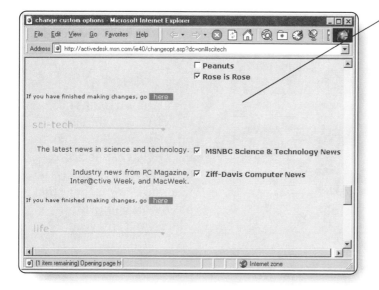

28. **Make changes** to your desktop component.

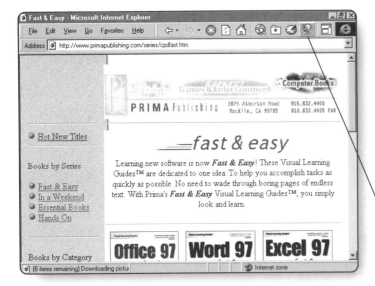

SURFING THROUGH THE CHANNELS

After you have selected the channels that you want to have on your desktop, you will want to try them out. Follow the steps outlined next and have a look.

1. **Click** on the **Channel button**. The Channel Bar will appear on the left side of the browser window.

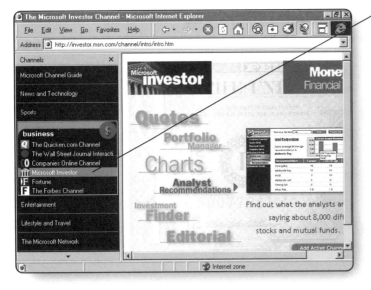

2. **Click** on a **channel icon**. The channel icon will be selected.

NOTE

Some channel icons take you directly to the sub-scription page for a channel. Other channel icons display a list of channels or take you to a Web page that has more channels from which you can select.

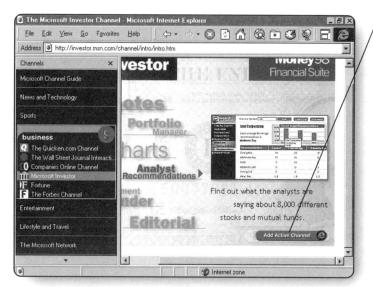

3. **Click** on the **Add Active Channel hyperlink**. The Modify Channel Usage dialog box will appear.

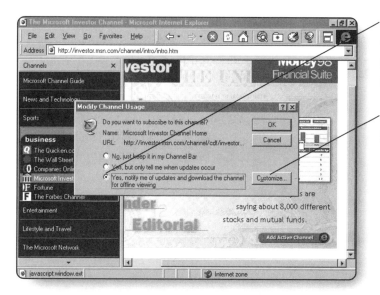

4. **Click** on an **option button** to specify how you want to subscribe to the channel. The option will be selected.

5. **Click** on **Customize**. The Subscription Wizard will appear.

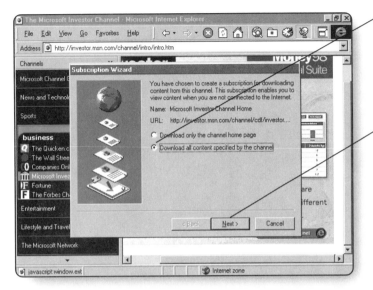

6. Click on the **option button** to specify how much channel content to download to your computer. The option will be selected.

7. Click on **Next**. The next page of the Wizard will appear.

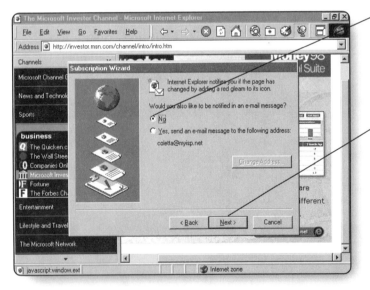

8. Click on an **option button** to specify how you want to be notified when channel content changes. The option will be selected.

9. Click on **Next**. The next page of the Wizard will appear.

NOTE
If you need to change the e-mail address, click on the Change Address button.

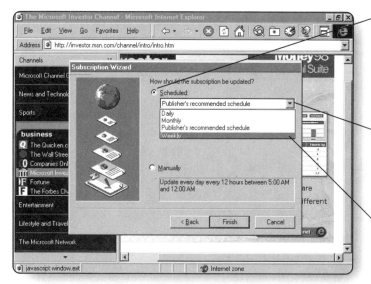

10. Click on an **option button** to specify how often Internet Explorer should check for updated content. The option will be selected.

11. Click on the **down arrow** (▼) on the Scheduled: drop-down list. A list of schedules will appear.

12. Click on the **schedule** you want to use. The schedule will be selected.

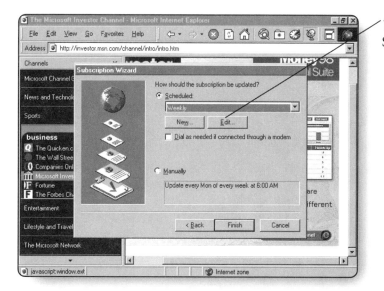

13. Click on **Edit**. The Custom Schedule dialog box will open.

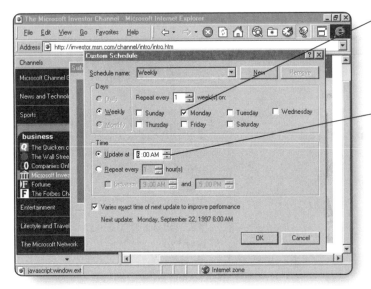

14. **Click** on the **day of the week** you want to check for updated content. A ✔ will appear next to the option.

15. **Click** on the **up** and **down arrows** (♦) to select the time of day to check for updated content .

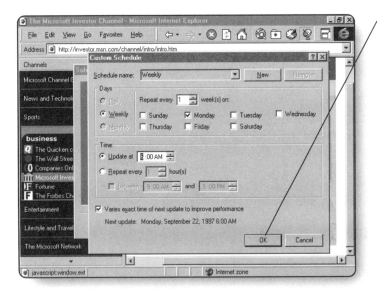

16. **Click** on **OK**. The Subscription Wizard will appear.

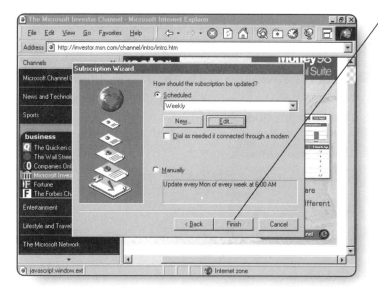

17. **Click** on **Finish**. The Modify Channel Usage dialog box will open.

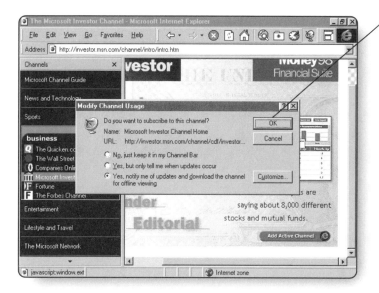

18. **Click** on **OK**. The channel will appear.

19. Continue reading the channel pages and clicking links until you don't want to explore the channel any longer.

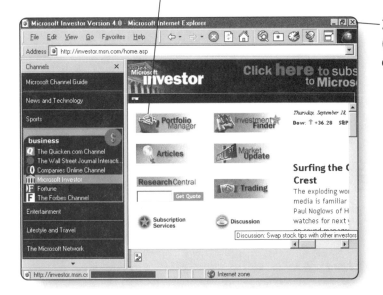

20. Click on the Close button ([×]). The Channel Viewer will close.

PART II REVIEW QUESTIONS

1. What are the four functions that the Explorer Bar performs? *See "Using the Explorer Bar" in Chapter 4.*

2. Where can you find a list of Web sites that you previously accessed by typing the URL into the Address Box? *See "Starting Your Adventure from the Address Box" in Chapter 4.*

3. If you have a Web page that you designed yourself that contains links to places you like to visit, how do you make this page your Start Page? *See "Choosing Your Own Start Page" in Chapter 5.*

4. How do you set up Internet Explorer so that it always says no to cookies? *See "Securing the Cookie Jar" in Chapter 5.*

5. How do you specify whether or not to download the content of a Web page to your computer? *See "Adding a Site to Your List of Favorites" in Chapter 6.*

6. How do you have Internet Explorer send you an e-mail message to notify you that a Web page has changed? *See "Subscribing to a Web Site" in Chapter 6.*

7. How can you find an e-mail address for a cousin that you haven't seen since you were a little kid? *See "Searching for People" in Chapter 7.*

8. What is the shortcut method of downloading files to your computer? *See "Using a Right-Click to Save Files" in Chapter 7.*

9. How can you set your own schedule for when to download content from a channel to which you have subscribed? *See "Surfing through the Channels" in Chapter 8.*

10. Can you add a Web page that you created and have stored on your computer to your desktop? *See "Adding Your Own Components to the Desktop" in Chapter 8.*

PART III

Managing Mail and News with Outlook Express

ozi

UPPO

plor
e

f the we

pecial D
Bringing Y

ush technology"
own—but what e
how Microsoft Int
push technology

9 What's on the Outlook Express Screen

Outlook Express is the new and improved version of Microsoft Internet Mail & News. If you've used Internet Mail & News before, this chapter will help you become familiar with the new look of Outlook Express. If you are new to mail and news programs, this chapter will guide you on a visual tour of how Outlook Express works. You'll also learn a few shortcuts along the way. In this chapter, you'll learn how to:

✦ Manage files and folders

✦ Change the look of the Outlook Express screen

✦ Personalize your messages

✦ Move around in newsgroups

NAVIGATING THROUGH THE MENUS

This section will give you a basic understanding of some of the menu commands that are unique to Outlook Express.

Creating a New Folder

When your Inbox and Outbox start to contain so many messages that keeping track of them is hard, you can create additional folders in which to file your messages.

1. **Click** on **File**. The File menu will appear.

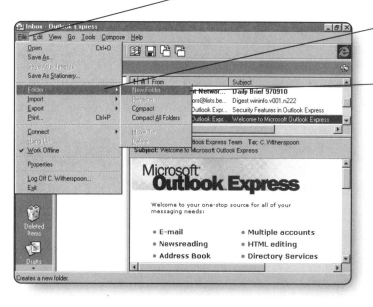

2. **Click** on **Folder**. A cascading menu will appear.

3. **Click** on **New Folder**. The Create Folder dialog box will open.

4. **Type** a **name** for the new folder in the Folder name: text box.

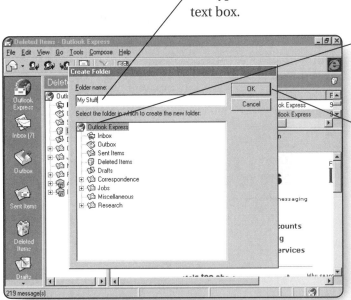

5. **Click** on the **folder** into which you want to place the subfolder. The folder will be selected.

6. **Click** on **OK**. Your new folder will appear in the list of Outlook Express folders.

Getting Rid of Wasted Space

When you move messages around and delete messages, you accumulate wasted space in your mailbox. Usually, Outlook Express will prompt you when it is time to get rid of this wasted space. Here's how you can manually compact your mailbox.

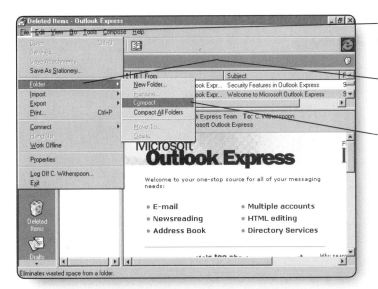

1. **Click** on **File**. The File menu will appear.

2. **Click** on **Folder**. A cascading menu will appear.

3. **Click** on **Compact**. A dialog box will open while Outlook Express is getting rid of the extra space in all of your folders.

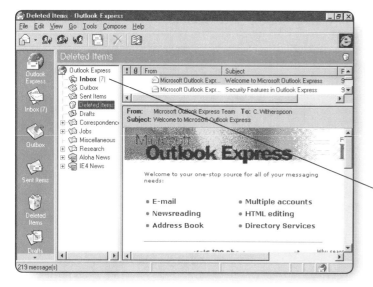

Finding Messages

If you don't want to scroll through lists of messages to find the one you need, use this quick search shortcut to find just what you're looking for.

1. Click on the **folder** you want to search. The folder will be selected.

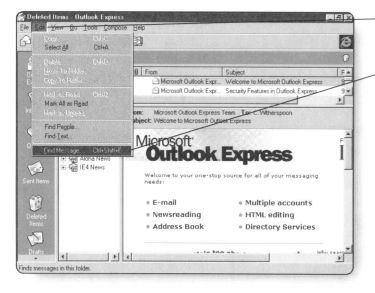

2. Click on **Edit**. The Edit menu will appear.

3. Click on **Find Message**. The Find Message dialog box will open.

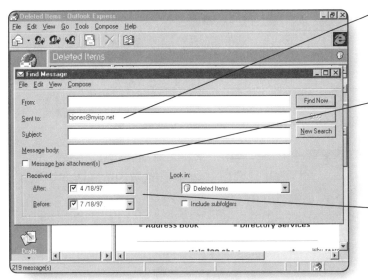

4. Type the **e-mail address** in the Sent to: text box of the message that you want to look for.

5. Click on **Message has attachment(s)** if the message you are looking for has an attachment. A ✔ will appear in the box.

6. Click on the **down arrows** (▼) next to the After: and Before: list boxes. A calendar will appear.

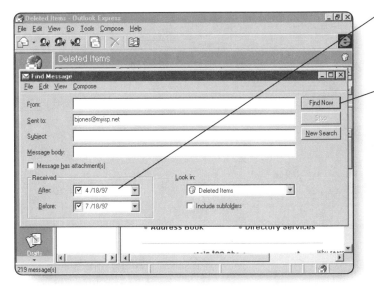

7. Click on a **date range** for the message. The date range will be selected.

8. Click on the **Find Now button**. Outlook Express will search for the message and highlight any matching messages in the message list.

Viewing Messages

You can view how messages display in the message list in several different ways. Experiment until you find a way that works best for you.

1. **Click** on **View**. The View menu will appear.

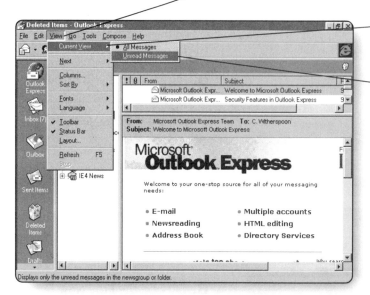

2. **Click** on **Current View**. A cascading menu will appear.

3. **Click** on **Unread Messages**. Only messages that you have not read will appear in the message list.

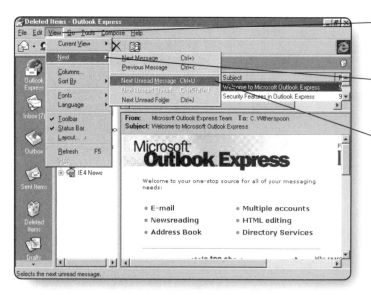

4. **Click** on **View**. The View menu will appear.

5. **Click** on **Next**. A cascading menu will appear.

6. **Click** on **Next Unread Message**. The next unread message in the folder will be selected in the message list and the message will display in the preview area.

Viewing Message Headers

You can choose how much information about a message to display in the message list. Take a look at the type of information you can display and decide what would be the most useful for you.

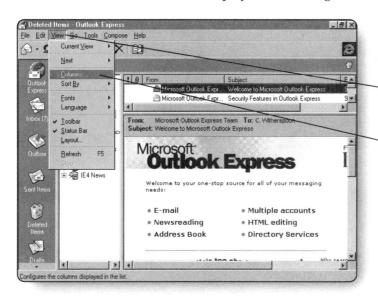

1. **Click** on **View**. The View menu will appear.

2. **Click** on **Columns**. The Columns dialog box will open.

3. **Click** on the **type** of information you want to add to the message list columns in the Available columns: box. The item will be selected.

4. **Click** on **Add**. The column will be added to the message list.

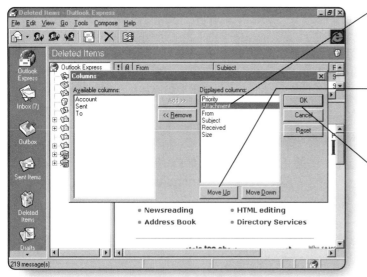

5. **Click** on the **column** that you want to move. The item will be selected.

6. **Click** on the **Move Up button**. The item will be moved one column to the left.

7. **Click** on **OK**. The dialog box will close.

Moving between Folders

If you don't want to use the Folder List or the Folder Bar, you can still move between folders.

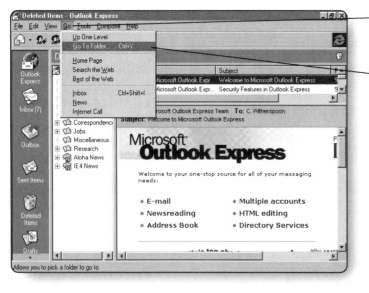

1. **Click** on **Go**. The Go menu will appear.

2. **Click** on **Go To Folder**. The Go To Folder dialog box will open.

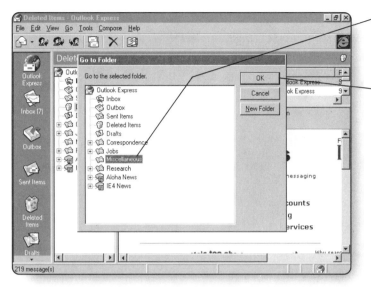

3. **Click** on the **folder** that you want to open. The folder will be selected.

4. **Click** on **OK**. The folder that you selected will display in the Outlook Express screen.

Choosing a Stationery

Stationery adds a unique look to all of your correspondence. You can use the stationery that comes with Outlook Express or you can design your own. You can also add a signature or a business card to your messages. Signature files give your messages a standard close. Business cards make it easy for people you correspond with to add your address information to their Windows Address Book.

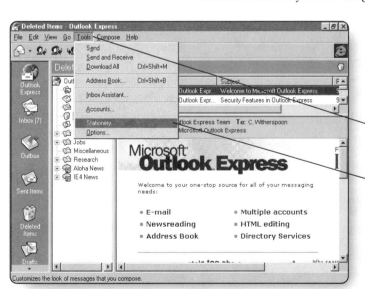

1. **Click** on **Tools**. The Tools menu will appear.

2. **Click** on **Stationery**. The Stationery dialog box will open.

3. Click on the **Mail** or **News tab** to select the type of account for which you're creating stationery.

4. Click on the **This stationery option**. The option will be selected.

5. Click on **Select**. The Select Stationery dialog box will open.

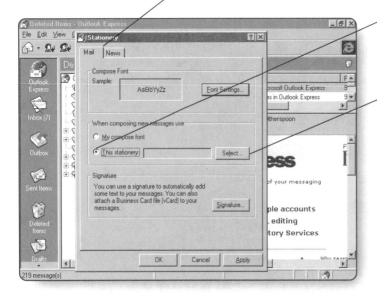

6. Click on the **stationery** you want to use. The stationery will be selected.

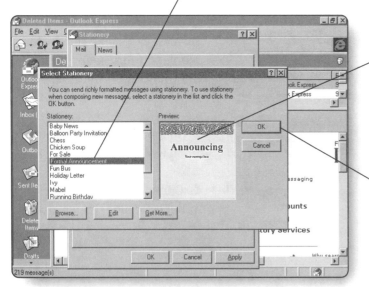

NOTE

When you click on a stationery, a preview of what the stationery looks like will appear in the preview area.

7. Click on **OK**. The selected stationery will show as a background in all messages you send and the Stationery dialog box will open.

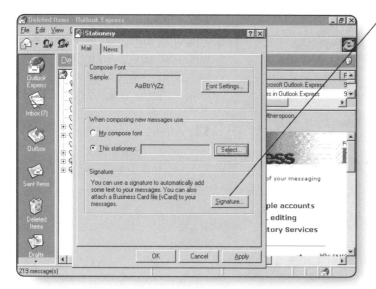

8. Click on **Signature**. The Signature dialog box will open.

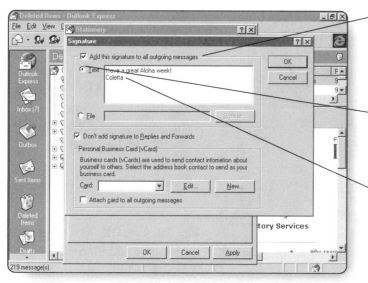

9. Click on **Add this signature to all outgoing messages**. A ✔ will appear in the box, indicating that it is selected.

10. Click on the **Text option**. The option to use a text signature will be selected.

11. Type a **signature**. This signature will appear at the end of all your outgoing messages.

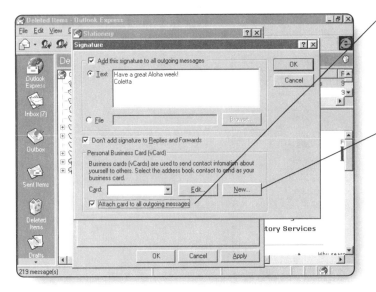

12. **Click** on **Attach card to all outgoing messages** to attach a business card to your outgoing e-mail messages. A ✔ will appear in the box.

13. **Click** on **New**. The Contact Properties dialog box will open.

14. **Type** as much **information** about yourself as you want to appear in your business card.

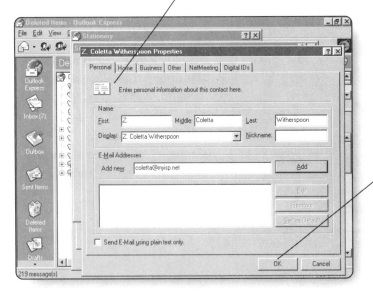

NOTE

For directions of how to use the Contact Properties sheet, see the section titled "Adding Contacts to the Address Book" in Chapter 11.

15. **Click** on **OK**. Your business card will be added to the Windows Address Book.

16. Click on the **down arrow** (▼) to the right of the Card: list box. A list of business cards will appear.

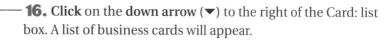
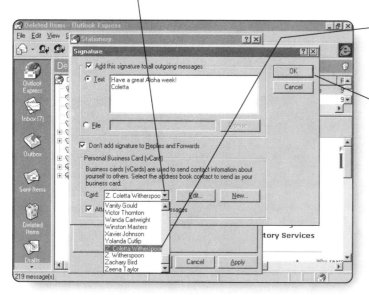

17. Click on your **business card** from the list. Your business card will be selected.

18. Click on **OK**. Your signature and business card will automatically be included in all your outgoing messages.

Setting Outlook Express Options

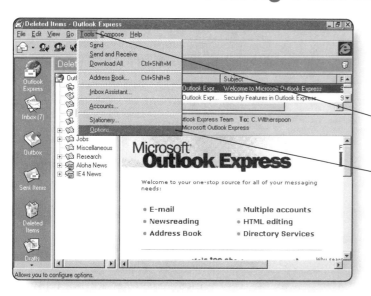

You may want to change how you work with Outlook Express. You can do this from one convenient place.

1. Click on **Tools**. The Tools menu will appear.

2. Click on **Options**. The Options dialog box will open with the General tab at the top of the stack.

3. Click on **Check for new messages every … minutes**. A ✔ will appear in the box.

4. Type the **interval** that you want Outlook Express to check messages.

5. Click on **Empty messages from 'Deleted Items' folder on exit**. A ✔ will appear in the box.

6. Click on **When starting, go directly to my 'Inbox' folder**. A ✔ will appear in the box.

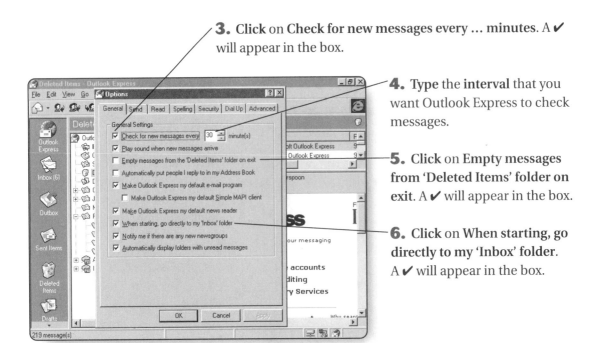

7. Click on the **Send tab**. The Send tab will come to the top of the stack.

8. Click on the **option** for the format that you want to use for your e-mail messages in the News sending format area. The option will be selected.

9. Click on **Save copy of sent messages in the 'Sent Items' folder** to automatically save a copy of all your outgoing correspondence. A ✔ will appear in the box.

10. Click on **Include message in reply** to have the original message quoted in your reply message. A ✔ will appear in the box.

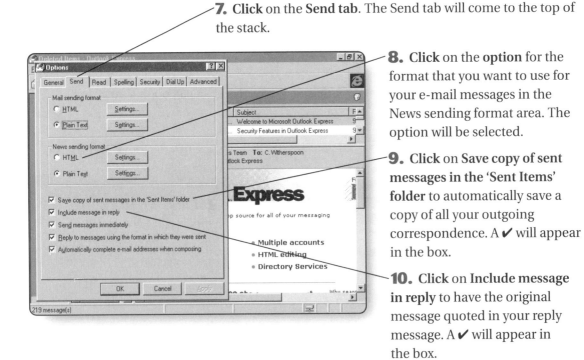

11. **Click** on the **Read tab.** The Read tab will come to the top of the stack.

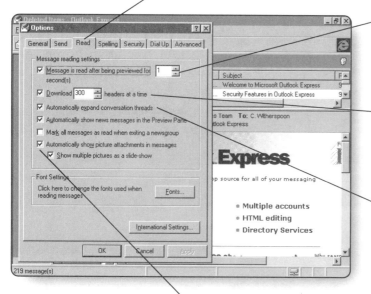

12. **Click** on the **up and down arrows** (♦) to select the amount of time to elapse before marking a message as being read.

13. **Click** on the **up and down arrows** (♦) to select the number of message headers to download at one time.

14. **Click** on **Automatically expand conversation thread** to automatically display all messages in a message thread. A ✔ will appear in the box.

15. **Click** on **Automatically show picture attachments in messages** to show picture attachments in the message preview pane. A ✔ will appear in the box.

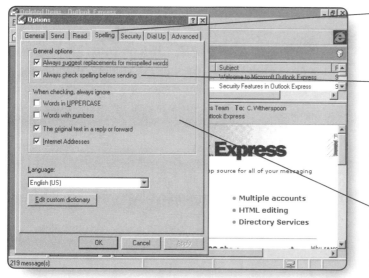

16. **Click** on the **Spelling tab**. The Spelling tab will come to the top of the stack.

17. **Click** on **Always check spelling before sending** to have Outlook Express perform a spell check on your message before you send it. A ✔ will appear in the box.

18. **Click** on the **items** that you do not want Outlook Express to spell check in the When checking, always ignore area. A ✔ will appear in the boxes you selected.

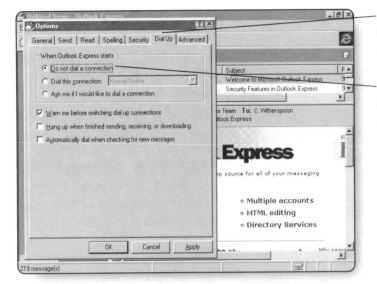

19. Click on the **Dial Up tab**. The Dial Up tab will come to the top of the stack.

20. Click on the **option button** that corresponds to the way you want Outlook Express to make a connection when it opens. The option will be selected.

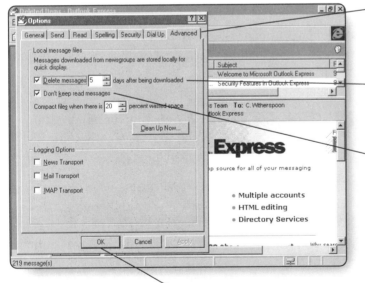

21. Click on the **Advanced tab**. The Advanced tab will come to the top of the stack..

22. Type the **number of days** you would like to keep messages stored on your computer.

23. Click on **Don't keep read messages** to delete read news messages on your computer. A ✔ will appear in the box.

24. Click on **OK**. Your new option settings will be applied.

TAKING ADVANTAGE OF TOOLBARS

Toolbar buttons provide a shortcut to the most commonly used menu commands. Remember, if you are unsure what task a button performs, just hold the mouse pointer over the button and a screen tip will appear.

Saving Messages

Sometimes you would rather save a message than move it to a different folder inside Outlook Express. By saving a message, you can also change the file format. This makes opening the file in other software programs easier.

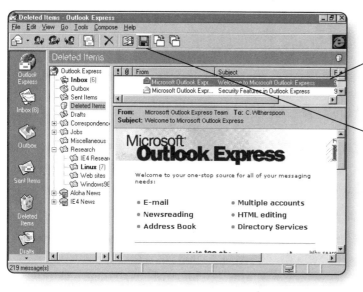

1. **Click** on the **message** that you want to save. The message will be selected.

2. **Click** on the **Save button**. The Save Message As dialog box will open.

3. **Select** the **folder** in which you want to store the message. The folder will be selected.

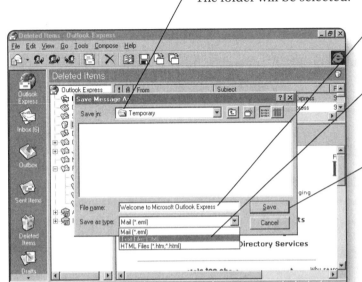

4. **Type** a **name** for the file in the File name: text box.

5. **Select** the **format** in which you want to have the file saved. The format will be selected.

6. **Click** on **Save**. The message will be saved to the designated folder.

Moving Messages

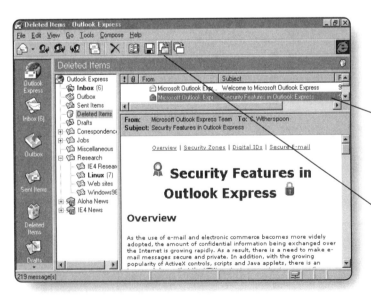

When you are organizing your messages, use the Move To button to make the task a little easier.

1. **Click** on the **message** that you want to move to a different folder. The message will be selected.

2. **Click** on the **Move To button**. The Move dialog box will open.

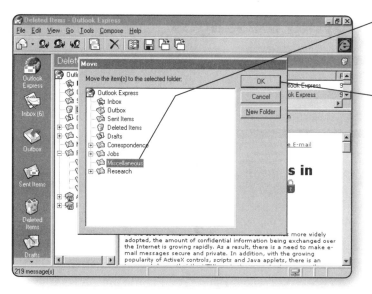

3. Click on the **folder** to which you want to move the message. The folder will be selected.

4. Click on **OK**. The message will be moved to the designated folder.

Deleting Messages

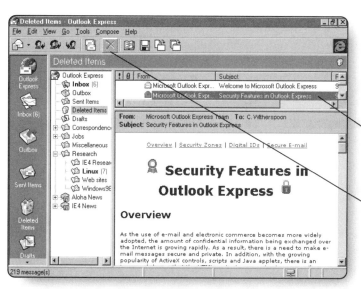

When you just don't want to keep old messages around any longer, you can remove them and send them to the Deleted Items folder.

1. Click on the **message** that you want to remove. The message will be selected.

2. Click on the **Delete button**. The message will be sent to the Deleted Items folder.

Copying Messages

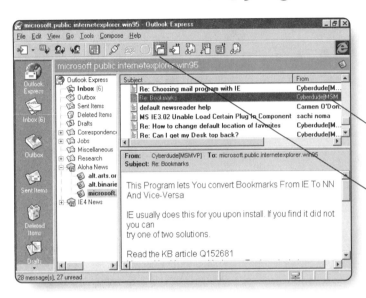

When you're lurking in the newsgroups and you find a piece of information that you can use, make yourself a copy for later use.

1. Click on the **message** that you want to copy. The message will be selected.

2. Click on the **Copy To button**. The Copy dialog box will open.

3. Click on the **folder** in which you want to place the copied message. The folder will be selected.

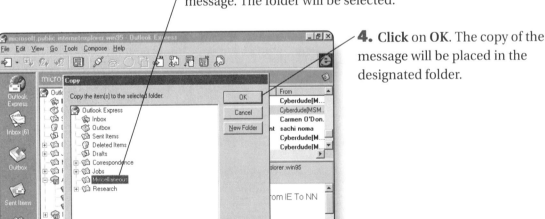

4. Click on **OK**. The copy of the message will be placed in the designated folder.

Navigating between Messages

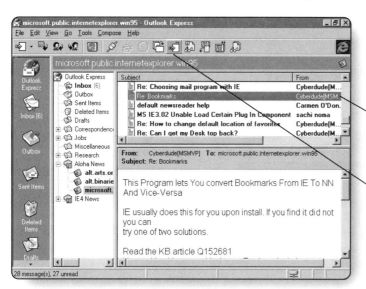

There are lots of ways to move from message to message and newsgroup to newsgroup. Here's a short tour to get you moving.

1. Click on a **message** to read it. The message will appear in the preview pane.

2. Click on the **Next Unread Message button**. The next message in the message list that you have not read will appear in the message preview pane.

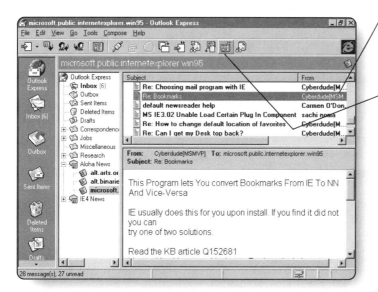

3. Click on a **message** to read it. The message will appear in the preview pane.

4. Click on the **Next Unread Newsgroup button**. The next newsgroup that has unread messages will download and the first unread message will display in the message preview pane.

Marking Messages as Being Read

If there is a conversation topic that just doesn't interest you and you don't want to see those headers each time you go to that particular newsgroup, you can mark those messages as read.

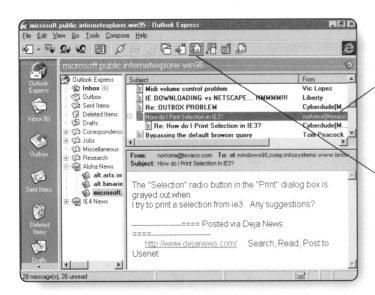

1. **Click** on a **message** that is part of the thread you want to mark as being read. The message will be selected.

2. **Click** on the **Mark Thread as Read button**. The messages will be marked as read without your having to view them.

3. **Click** on any **message** in a newsgroup. The message will be selected.

4. **Click** on the **Mark All as Read button**. All of the messages in the newsgroup will be marked as read without your having to view them.

Downloading Newsgroup Messages

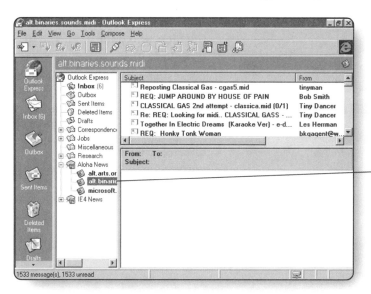

If you don't want to keep your phone line occupied while you browse through your newsgroups, download them to your computer. You can read the messages later without tying up the phone.

1. **Click** on the **newsgroup** that you want to download. The headers for all of the unread messages will download to your computer.

2. **Click** on the **Download Newsgroup button**. The Download Newsgroup dialog box will open.

3. Click on **Get the following items:** to select the newsgroup content to download. A ✔ will appear in the box.

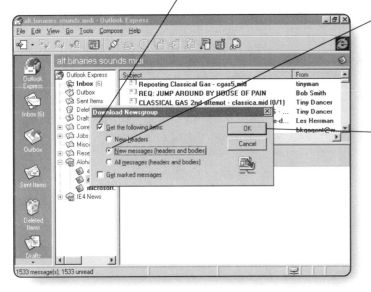

4. Click on the **New messages (headers and bodies) option** to download message headers and bodies. The option will be selected.

5. Click on **OK**. All of the messages for the selected newsgroup will be downloaded to your computer.

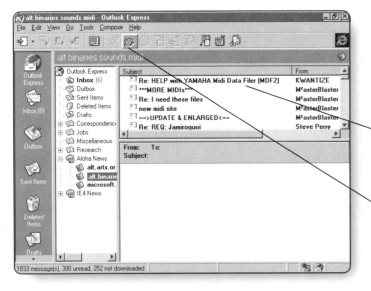

Disconnecting

When you're done downloading all of those messages, it's time to close your Internet connection.

1. **Download messages** while you are connected to a news server.

2. Click on the **Hang Up button**. You will be disconnected from your Internet connection.

REVIEWING SCREEN ELEMENTS

Outlook Express gives you several tools to work with on the screen. You can pick and choose between the ones you want to use. Experiment with each tool and use the ones that are most comfortable for you.

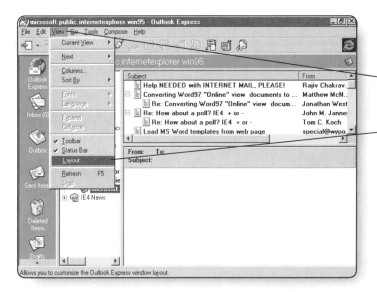

1. **Click** on **View**. The View menu will appear.

2. **Click** on **Layout**. The Window Layout Properties dialog box will open.

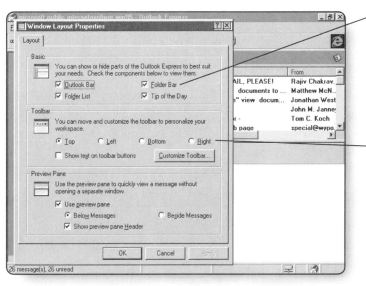

3. **Click** on the **screen elements** in the Basic area that you want to display in the Outlook Express window. A ✔ will appear in the box next to the elements you selected.

4. **Click** on the **option button** in the Toolbar area that corresponds to where you want to locate the Toolbar. The option will be selected.

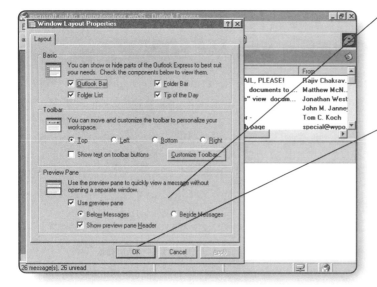

5. **Click** on the **option button** in the Preview Pane area to select where to place the message preview pane. The option will be selected.

6. **Click** on **OK**. The Outlook Express window will display with a new look.

10 Handling E-mail

Electronic mail (or e-mail) is one of the very first things that people used computer networks for, and it is still the most popular application used on the Internet. E-mail is an easy, fast, and inexpensive way to keep in contact with friends, relatives, and colleagues. In this chapter, you'll learn how to:

✦ Set up Outlook Express to handle e-mail and newsgroups

✦ Send and receive messages

✦ Attach files to your e-mail message

✦ Add HTML formatting to your messages

SETTING UP A MAIL ACCOUNT

Before you can begin sending and receiving e-mail, you need to set up Outlook Express so that it can communicate with your ISP.

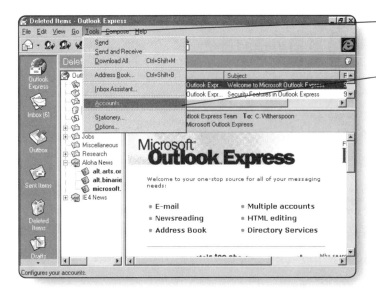

1. **Click** on **Tools**. The Tools menu will appear.

2. **Click** on **Accounts**. The Internet Accounts dialog box will open.

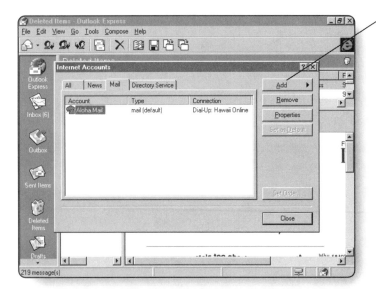

3. **Click** on **Add**. A cascading menu will appear.

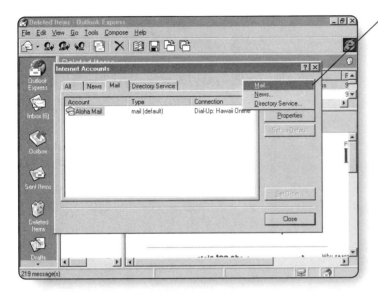

4. Click on **Mail**. The Internet Connection Wizard will start.

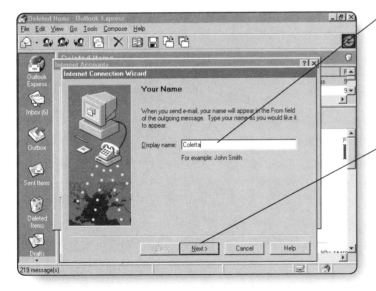

5. Type your **name** in the Display Name: text box. The way you type it here is how your name will appear in the header information of your outgoing messages.

6. Click on **Next**. The Internet E-mail Address dialog box will open.

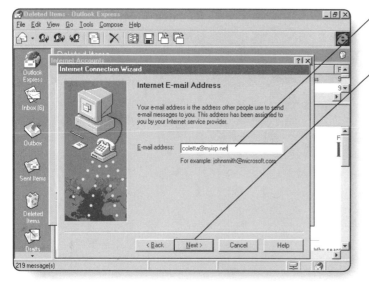

7. Type your **e-mail address** in the E-mail Address: text box.

8. Click on **Next**. The E-mail Server Names dialog box will open.

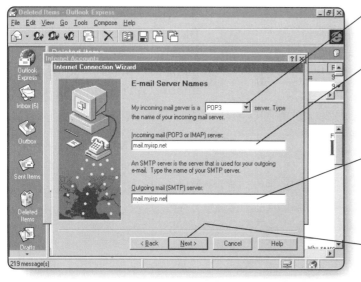

9. Select or type the **e-mail server** used by your ISP.

10. Type the **name** of your ISP's incoming mail server in the Incoming mail (POP3 or IMAP) server: text box.

11. Type the **name** of your ISP's outgoing mail server in the Outgoing mail (SMTP) server: text box.

12. Click on **Next**. The Internet Mail Logon dialog box will open.

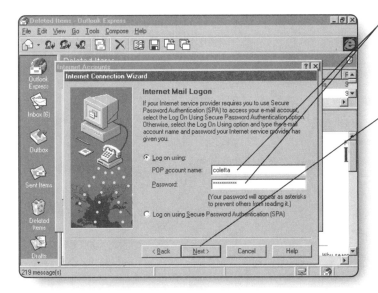

13. **Type** your **username** and **password,** as provided by your ISP, in the POP account name: and Password: text boxes.

14. **Click** on **Next**. The Friendly Name dialog box will open.

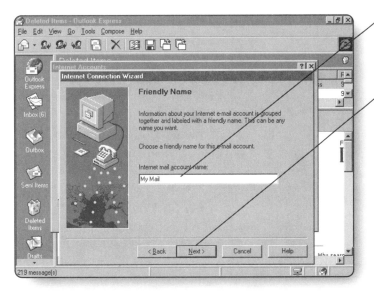

15. **Type** a **name** in the Internet mail account name: text box to identify your e-mail account.

16. **Click** on **Next**. The Choose Connection Type dialog box will open.

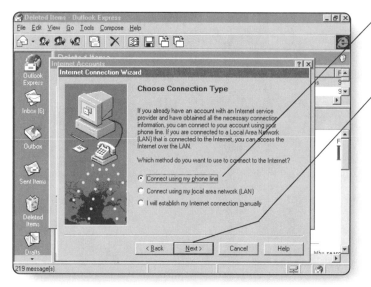

17. **Click** on the **option** that you use to connect to the Internet. The option will be selected.

18. **Click** on **Next**. The Choose Modem dialog box will open.

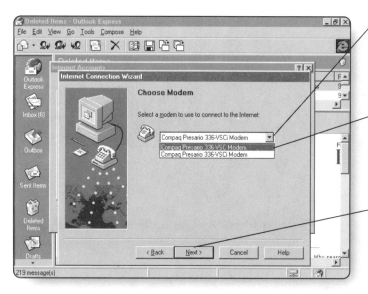

19. **Click** on the **down arrow** (▼) next to the Choose Modem list box. A drop-down list will appear.

20. **Click** on your **computer's modem** from the drop-down box. The modem will be selected.

21. **Click** on **Next**. The Dial-up Connection dialog box will open.

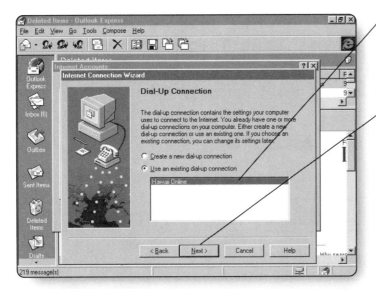

22. **Click** on the **connection** that you will be using to connect to your ISP's e-mail server. The connection will be selected.

23. **Click** on **Next**. The Congratulations dialog box will open.

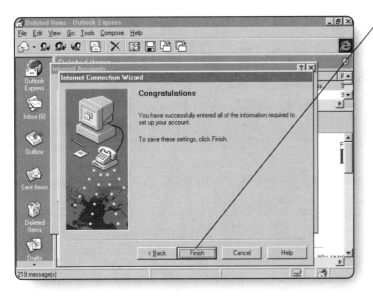

24. **Click** on **Finish**. You will be returned to the Internet Account dialog box.

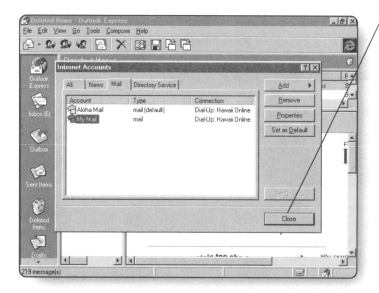

25. **Click** on **Close**. You will now be ready to receive e-mail.

RECEIVING MESSAGES

1. **Click** on the **Inbox icon**. The contents of your incoming mailbox will appear.

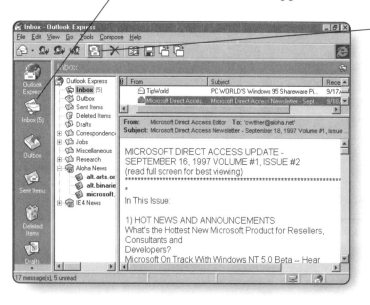

2. **Click** on the **Send and Receive button**. You will be connected to your ISP, and if you have any messages, they will be downloaded to your computer.

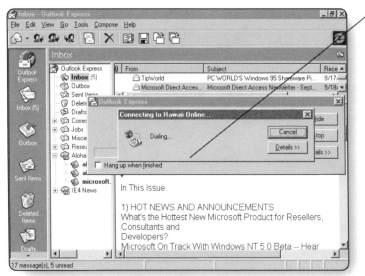

Outlook Express will automatically connect to your ISP.

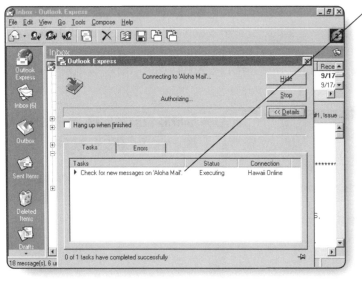

Outlook Express checks your ISP's mail server for new messages and begins the download process.

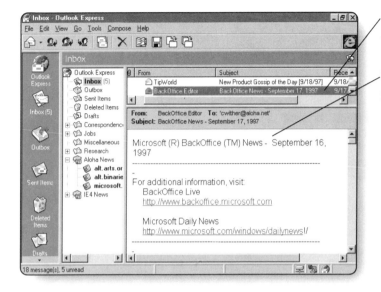

3. **Click** on the **message** that you want to read.

The message will display in the message pane.

SENDING MESSAGES

OK, now you know how to receive messages. In the following section, you will see how to send messages of your own and reply to e-mail that others send you.

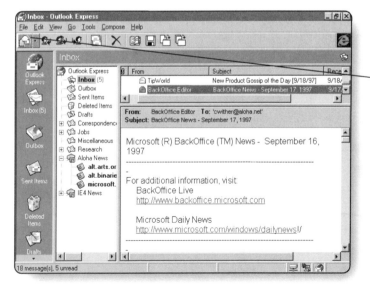

Sending a New Message

1. **Click** on the **New Message button**. A New Message window will appear.

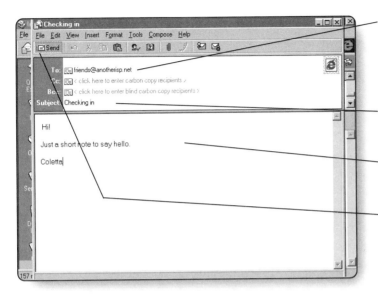

2. Type the **e-mail address** in the To: area of the person to whom you want to send the message.

3. Type a **subject** for your message in the Subject: area.

4. Type your **message** in the message pane.

5. Click on the **Send button**. A dialog box will open, telling you that your message will be placed in your Outbox.

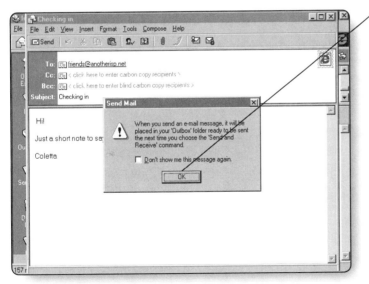

6. Click on **OK**. Your message will be ready to send.

7. Click on the **Outbox icon**. Your list of messages waiting to be sent will appear.

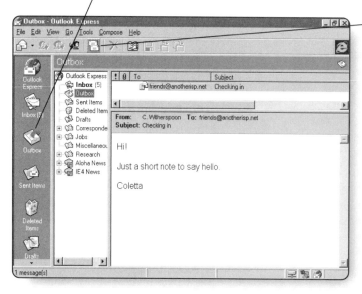

8. Click on the **Send and Receive button**. You will be connected to your ISP and your message will be sent to the designated e-mail address.

Replying to a Message

1. Click on the **Inbox icon**. The list of messages in your inbox will appear.

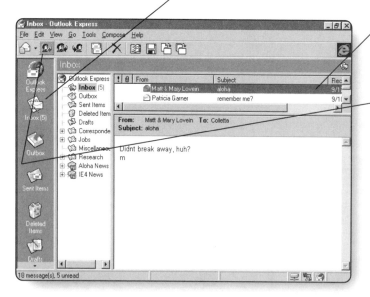

2. Click on the **message** to which you want to reply. The message will be selected.

3. Click on the **Reply to Author button**. A message window will appear with the address, subject, and original message displayed.

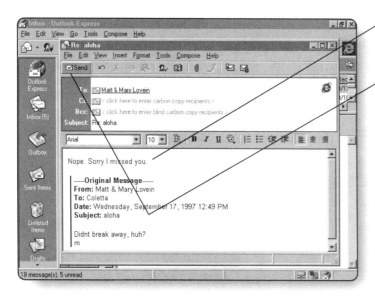

4. **Type** your **reply** in the message pane.

5. **Click** on the **Send button**. Your message will be placed in the Outbox and will be ready to send the next time you connect to your ISP.

Forwarding a Message

1. **Click** on the **Inbox icon**. Your list of received messages will appear.

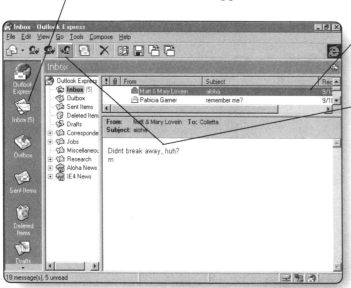

2. **Click** on the **message** that you want to forward. The message will be selected.

3. **Click** on the **Forward Message button**. A message window will appear with the subject and original message displayed.

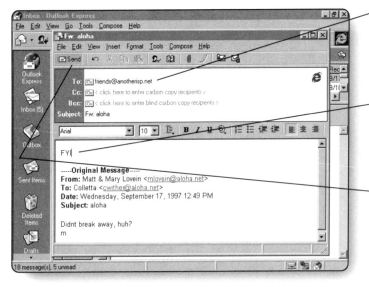

4. **Type** the **e-mail address** in the To: area of the person who is to receive the forwarded message.

5. **Type** a **message** in the message pane letting that person know what is being forwarded to him or her.

6. **Click** on the **Send button**. Your message will be placed in the Outbox and will be ready to send the next time you connect to your ISP.

SENDING ATTACHMENTS

Sometimes, when you send a message to someone, you will want to include a file. You can attach any kind of file to your message.

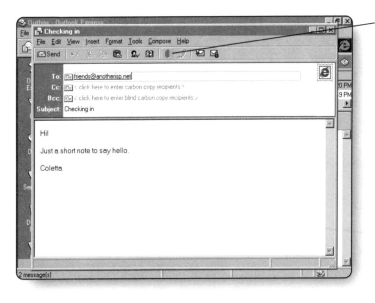

1. **Click** on the **Insert File button**. The Insert Attachment dialog box will open.

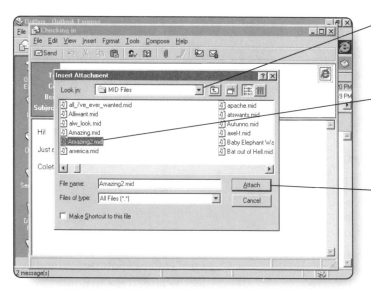

2. **Locate** the **directory** where the file that you want to attach is located. A list of files will appear.

3. **Click** on the **file** that you want to attach to your message. The filename will appear in the File name: text box.

4. **Click** on **Attach**. An icon will appear at the bottom of your message.

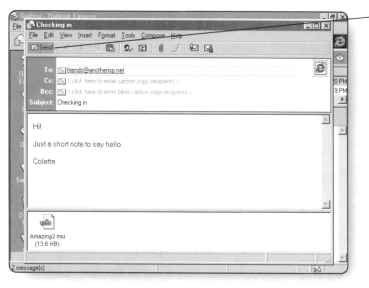

5. **Click** on the **Send button**. Your message will be placed in the Outbox and will be ready to send the next time you connect to your ISP.

FORMATTING YOUR MESSAGE

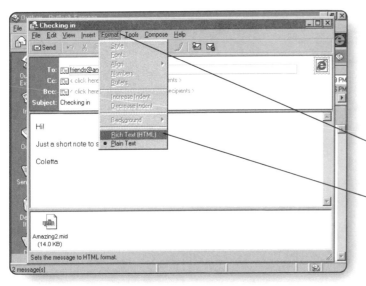

One of the newest additions to e-mail is the ability to add HTML formatting to messages. Now you can make your e-mail message look just like a Web page.

1. Click on **Format**. The Format menu will appear.

2. Click on **Rich Text (HTML)**. An HTML formatting toolbar will be added to the new message window.

3. Select the **text** that you want to format.

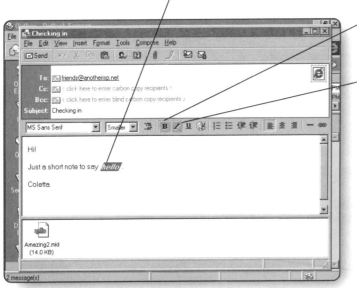

4. Click on the **Bold button**. The text will be bolded.

5. Click on the **Italic button**. The text will be italicized.

TIP

A word of caution: Before you send an HTML-formatted e-mail message, make sure that the recipient of your message uses an e-mail program that supports HTML.

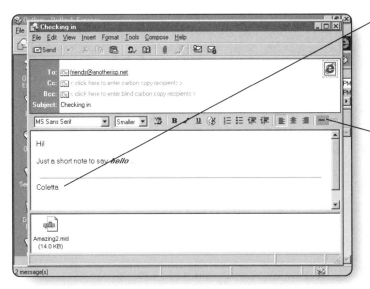

6. **Click before** the **text** where you want to add a horizontal line. The insertion point will move to the spot where you clicked.

7. **Click** on the **Insert Horizontal Line button**. A line will be added to your message.

8. **Click** on **Format**. The Format menu will appear.

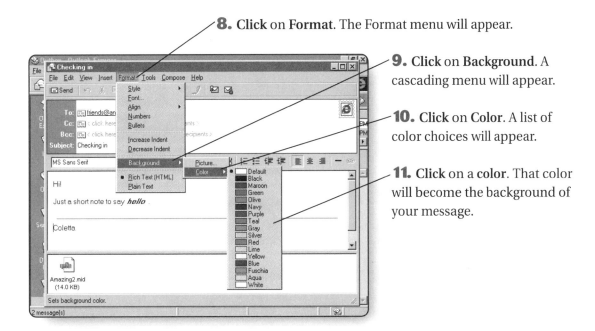

9. **Click** on **Background**. A cascading menu will appear.

10. **Click** on **Color**. A list of color choices will appear.

11. **Click** on a **color**. That color will become the background of your message.

11 Working with the Address Book

You will now see how to make the best use of the Windows address book to keep track of your contacts and make communicating with them easy. You can even import data from your old address books as well. Learning how to make good use of the address book features will make the job of keeping up your contacts with groups and individuals a snap. In this chapter, you'll learn how to:

✦ Use the Windows Address Book to keep track of your contacts

✦ Group your contacts to make mailings easier

✦ Print the contents of your address book

✦ Import and export address books

ADDING CONTACTS TO THE ADDRESS BOOK

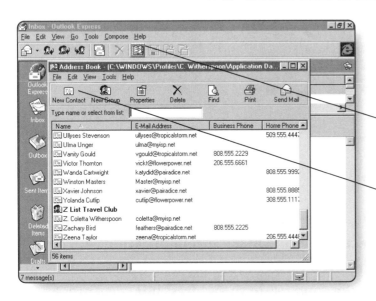

Adding new names to your address book is as simple as clicking on a button or two and filling in the dialog box.

1. **Click** on the **Address Book button**. The Windows Address Book will appear.

2. **Click** on the **New Contact button**. The Contact Properties dialog box will open and the Personal tab will be on top.

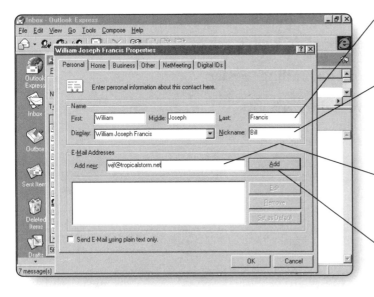

3. **Type** the **full name** of your contact in the First:, Middle:, and Last: text boxes.

4. **Type** a **nickname** for your contact in the Nickname: text box. Use a name that is easy for you to remember.

5. **Type** the **e-mail address** for your contact in the Add new: text box.

6. **Click** on **Add**. Your contact's e-mail address will be added to the list of e-mail addresses.

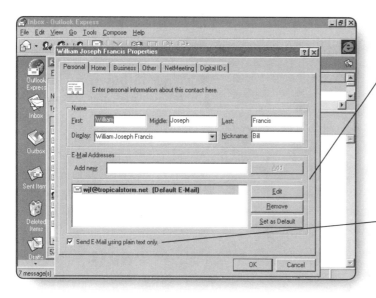

NOTE

You can enter multiple e-mail addresses for a single contact. Use the Edit, Remove, and Set as Default buttons to manage a contact's list of e-mail addresses.

7. Click on **Send E-Mail Using Plain Text Only** if your contact uses a mail program that does not read HTML-formatted messages. A ✔ will appear in the box.

8. Click on the **Home tab**. The Home tab will come to the top of the stack.

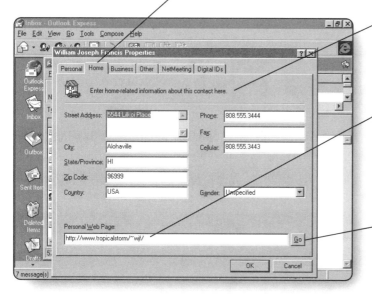

9. Type the **address** and **telephone information** for your contact in the corresponding text boxes.

10. Type the **URL** for your contact's personal Web page in the Personal Web Page: text box.

NOTE

If you are connected to the Internet, click on the Go button to visit your contact's Web page. Internet Explorer will open and your contact's Web page will be accessed.

11. Click on the **Business tab**. The Business tab will come to the top of the stack.

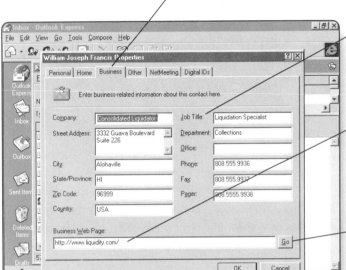

12. Type the **business address** and **telephone information** for your contact in the corresponding text boxes.

13. Type the **URL** of your contact's business Web page in the Business Web Page: text box.

NOTE

If you are connected to the Internet, click on the Go button to visit your contact's Web page. Internet Explorer will open and your contact's Web page will be accessed.

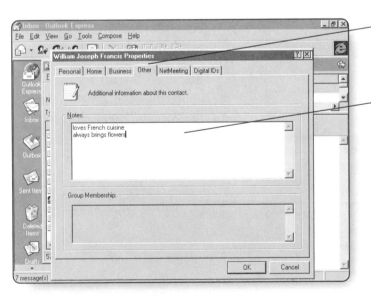

14. Click on the **Other tab**. The Other tab will come to the top of the stack.

15. Type **information** in the Notes: text box about your contact that you want to keep handy.

16. **Click** on the **NetMeeting tab**. The NetMeeting tab will come to the top of the stack.

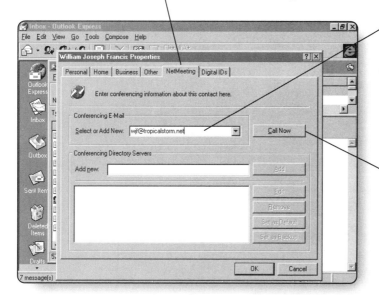

17. **Type** the **e-mail address or DNS number** in the Select or Add New: box where you can reach your contact for a NetMeeting conference call.

NOTE

If you are connected to the Internet, click on the Call Now button to start NetMeeting and call your contact to establish a conference.

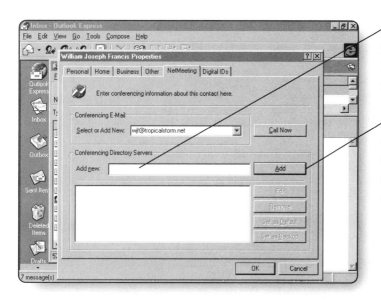

18. **Type** the **address** in the Add new: text box of a Conferencing Directory Server that you will use to call your contact.

19. **Click** on **Add**. The Conferencing Directory Server will be added to the list of servers that you can use to call your contact.

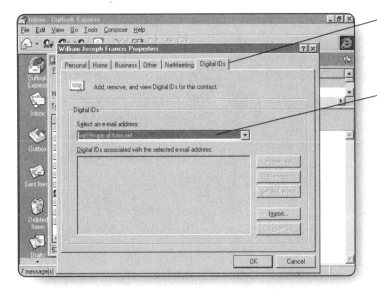

20. **Click** on the **Digital IDs tab**. The Digital IDs tab will come to the top of the stack.

21. **Select** the **e-mail address** that you want to associate with a digital ID.

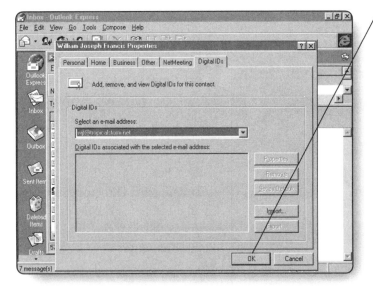

22. **Click** on **OK**. The Properties dialog box will close and your contact will be added to the Windows Address Book.

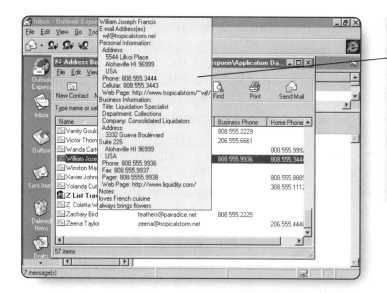

TIP

If you want to see all of the information on a contact but you don't want to open the Properties dialog box, place the mouse pointer over the contact's entry in the Address Book until a screen tip appears.

FORMING A GROUP

In many cases, you will find that organizing your contacts into groups, by job, organization, interests, and so on to be a great help. Mailing lists can be managed much more easily that way.

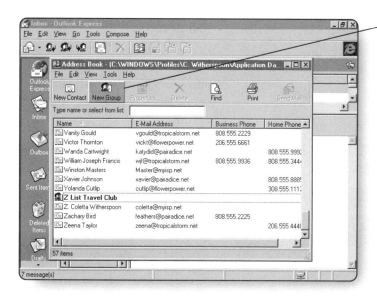

1. Click on the **New Group button**. The Group Properties dialog box will open.

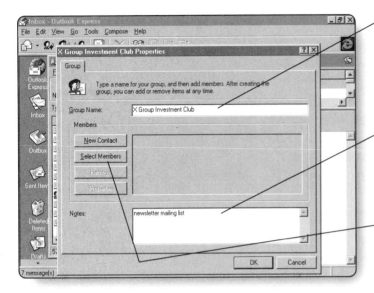

2. Type a **name** in the Group Name: text box for the group that you are creating. Use a name that describes the group or its function.

3. Type a **brief description** of the group in the Notes: text box. This is a good place to keep some notes about the group.

4. Click on the **Select Members button**. The Select Group Members dialog box will open.

5. Click on the **name** of a contact in the Name area that you want to add to the list of group members. The name will be selected.

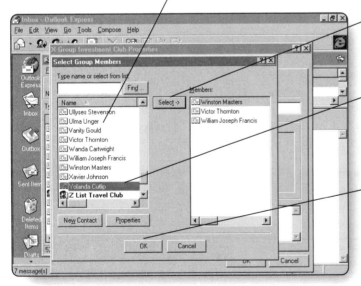

6. Click on **Select**. The contact's name will be added to the group Members: list.

7. Select additional **names** and **add** them to the list. The names you select will be added to the Members: list.

8. Click on **OK**. You will be returned to the Group Properties dialog box.

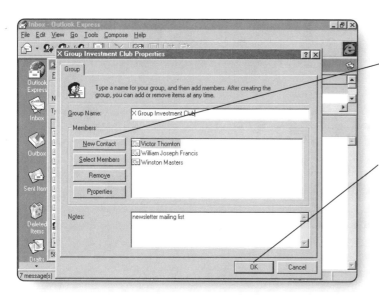

9. Click on **OK**. The group will be added to the address list.

PRINTING AN ADDRESS LIST

Occasionally, having a hard copy of your address list is nice. You can use the hard copy for a permanent file copy or to have with you when you are away from your desk. This can be very handy when you are traveling and working occasionally from a desk other than your own.

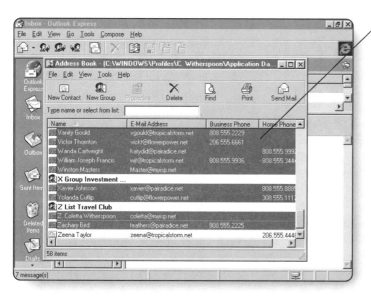

1. Select the **contacts** for which you want to print an address listing. The contacts will be selected.

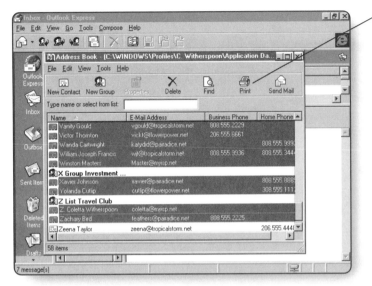

2. Click on the **Print button**. The Print dialog box will open.

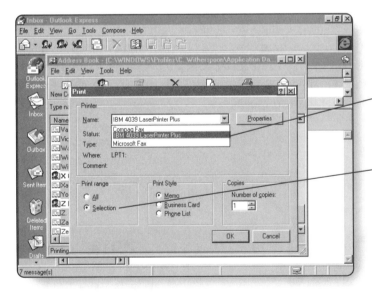

3. Click on the **down arrow** (▼) next to the Name: list box. A drop-down list will appear.

4. Click on a **printer** from the drop-down list. The printer will be selected.

5. Click on the **Selection option** to print only those contact names that were highlighted. The option will be selected.

TIP

If you want a complete printout of your address book, click on the All option button.

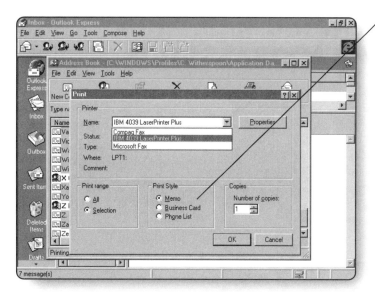

6. **Click** on one of the following **Print style options** for your address listing printout:

✦ The Memo style prints all the information in the address book.

✦ The Business Card style prints information that you would normally see on a business card.

✦ The Phone List style prints only phone numbers.

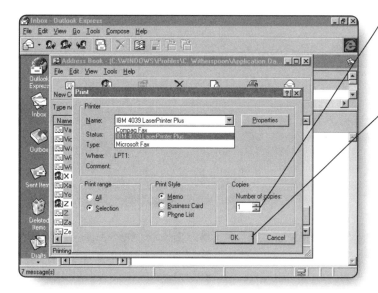

7. **Click** on the **up and down arrows** (◆) to select the number of copies of the address book that you want printed.

8. **Click** on **OK**. Your address list will begin to print.

SENDING MAIL FROM THE ADDRESS BOOK

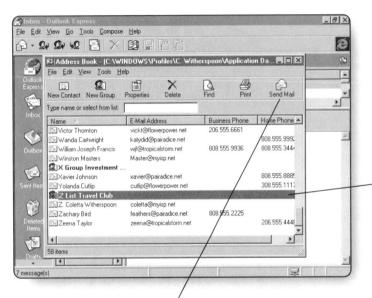

You can send mail directly from your address book. This feature comes in handy when you are checking over your lists for additional recipients for a message that you have already written or for one you need to compose.

1. Click on the **entry** for the contact to whom you want to send an e-mail message. The entry will be selected.

2. Click on the **Send Mail button**. A new message with the To: area addressed will appear.

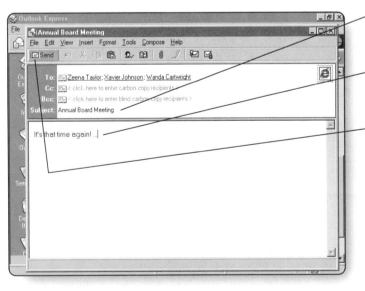

3. Type a **subject** for your message in the Subject: area.

4. Type your **message** in the message area.

5. Click on the **Send button**. Your message will be placed in your outbox until you connect to the Internet and send your messages.

IMPORTING AN ADDRESS BOOK

Importing other address books is simple to do. Perhaps you have upgraded to Internet Explorer 4.0 from a previous version and you wish to retain your address book listings, or maybe you have an address book from another mail program such as Eudora or Netscape.

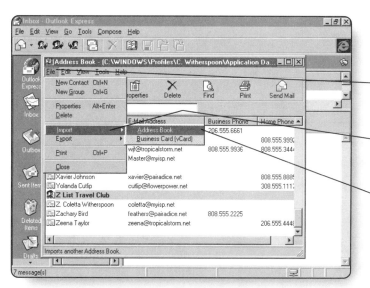

1. Click on **File**. The File menu will appear.

2. Click on **Import**. A cascading menu will appear.

3. Click on **Address Book**. The Windows Address Book Import Tool will appear.

4. Click on **the address book** that you want to import. The address book will be selected.

5. Click on the **Import button**. A dialog box will open, requesting file location information.

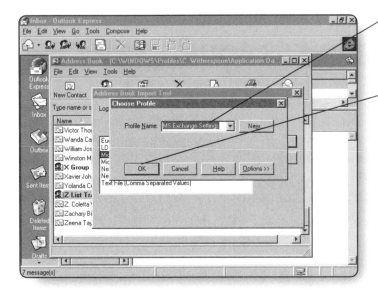

6. **Select** the **location** of the address book. The location will be selected.

7. **Click** on **OK**. The address book will be imported to the Windows Address book, and a dialog box will open.

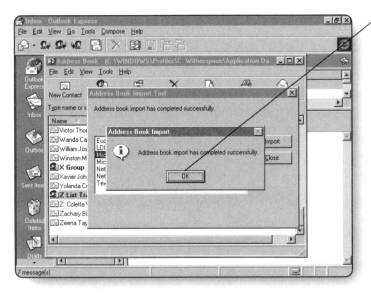

8. **Click** on **OK**. You will be returned to the Windows Address Book Import Tool dialog box.

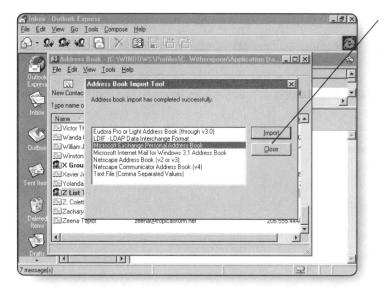

9. **Click** on **Close**. You will see the imported entries in the Windows Address Book.

EXPORTING AN ADDRESS BOOK

Exporting your address book is as easy as importing one.

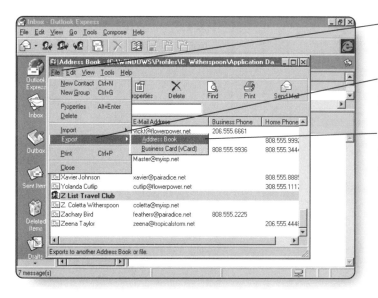

1. **Click** on **File**. The File menu will appear.

2. **Click** on **Export**. A cascading menu will appear.

3. **Click** on **Address Book**. The Windows Address Book Export Tool will appear.

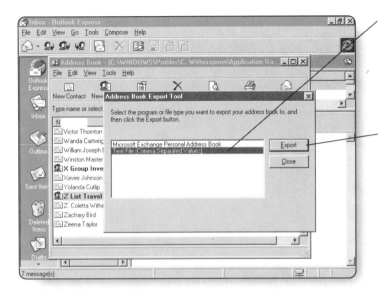

4. **Click** on **the address book** to which you want to export the Windows Address Book listing. The address book will be selected.

5. **Click** on **Export**. A dialog box will open, requesting file location information.

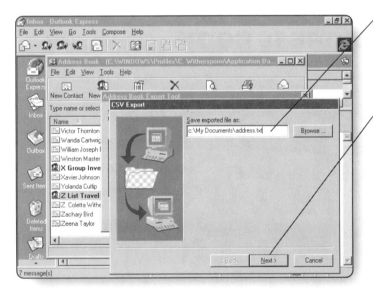

6. **Type** the **directory path** and a **filename** to which you want to export the Windows Address Book.

7. **Click** on **Next**. Another dialog box will open.

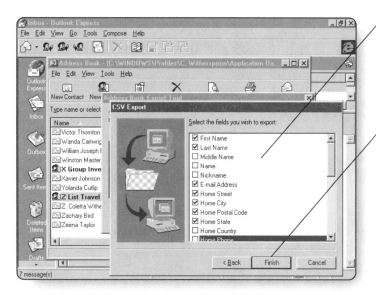

8. **Click** on each **field** that is associated with the information you want to export to the address book. A ✔ will appear next to the fields you selected.

9. **Click** on **Finish**. The address book will be exported, and a dialog box will open.

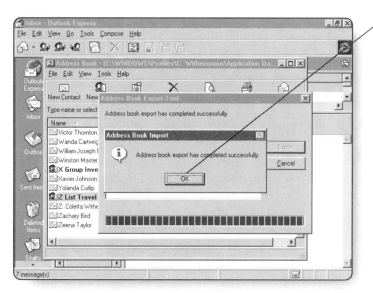

10. **Click** on **OK**. You will be returned to the Windows Address Book Export Tool dialog box.

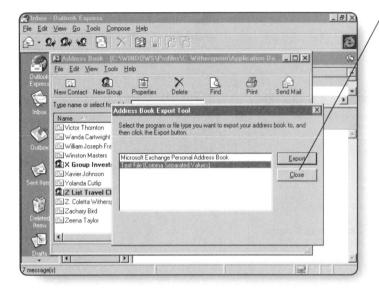

11. **Click** on **Close**. You will be returned to the Windows Address Book.

12 Participating in Newsgroup Discussions

Finding and joining one of the news "bulletin board" discussion groups on your favorite subject is easier than you think. With thousands of groups from which to choose, something is there for everyone. If you want to learn more about computers, check out the myriad computer-related newsgroups. You can usually find someone willing to help you solve a problem, answer a question on how to use a software program, or discuss the future of computers. If you're an inline skating fanatic and you want to talk with others who share your passion, look in the recreation newsgroups. Newsgroups are a great way to meet people. In this chapter, you'll learn how to:

✦ Set up a news server so that you can access newsgroups

✦ Subscribe to newsgroups

✦ Read and post messages in newsgroups

✦ Use newsgroup filters to limit the newsgroup messages

SETTING UP A NEWS ACCOUNT

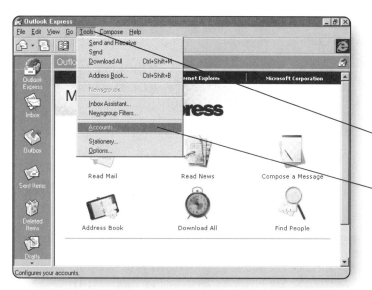

This section will guide you through the process of making the connection to your ISP and configuring network news on your machine.

1. **Click** on **Tools**. The Tools menu will appear.

2. **Click** on **Accounts**. The Internet Accounts dialog box will open.

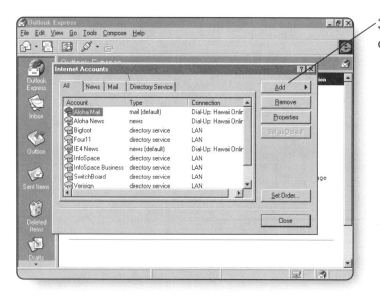

3. **Click** on **Add**. A menu of options will appear.

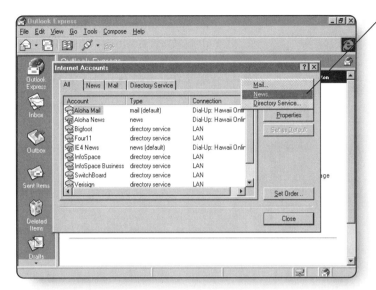

4. **Click** on **News**. The Internet Connection Wizard will appear with the Your Name screen displayed.

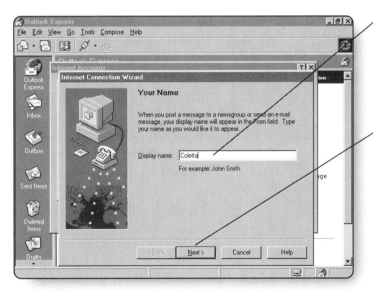

5. **Type** your **name** in the Display Name: text box. The way that you type your name is how you will be identified in newsgroup discussion threads.

6. **Click** on **Next**. The Internet News E-mail Address screen will appear.

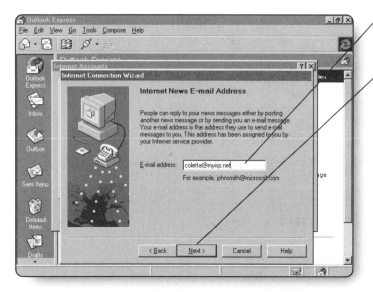

7. Type your **e-mail address** in the E-mail Address: text box.

8. Click on **Next**. The Internet News Server Name screen will appear.

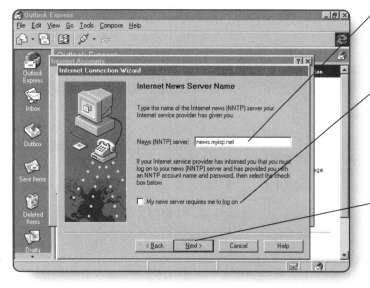

9. Type the **address** of your ISP's news server in the News (NNTP) server: text box.

10. Click on **My news server requires me to log on** if your ISP requires a username and password to access the news server. A ✔ will appear in the box.

11. Click on **Next**. The Friendly Name screen will appear.

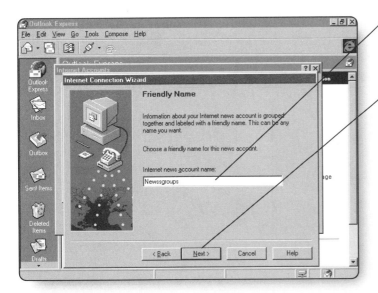

12. Type a **name** for your news account in the Internet news account name: text box.

13. Click on **Next**. The Choose Connection Type screen will appear.

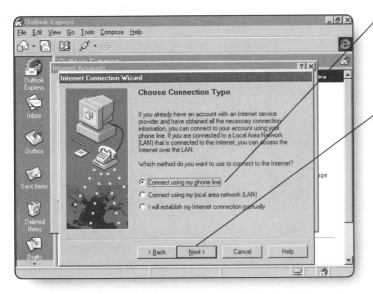

14. Click on the **option** for the method that you use to connect to the Internet. The option will be selected.

15. Click on **Next**. The Choose Modem screen will appear.

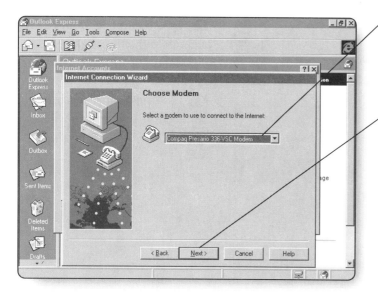

16. **Select** the **modem** that you use when you connect to the Internet. The modem will be selected.

17. **Click** on Next. The Dial-Up Connection screen will appear.

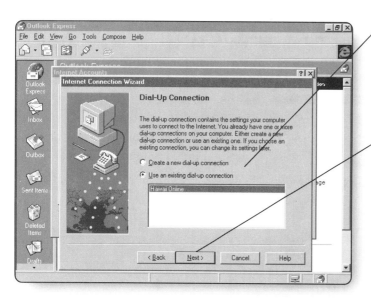

18. **Click** on the **dial-up connection** that Outlook Express will be using to access your ISP's news server. The dial-up connection option will be selected.

19. **Click** on Next. The Congratulations screen will appear.

NOTE

If you have not already set up a dial-up connection, click on the Create a new dial-up connection option. The wizard will take you through additional steps. You will need the access phone number, username, and password provided by your ISP.

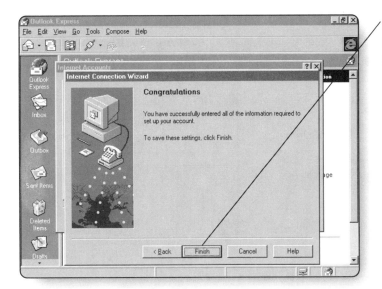

20. **Click** on **Finish**. You will return to the Internet Accounts dialog box.

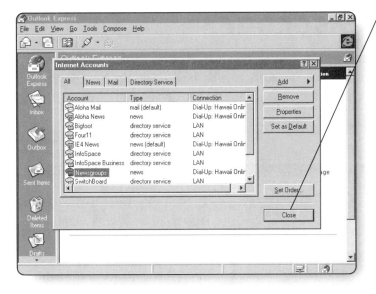

21. **Click** on **Close**. The news server will be added, Outlook Express will begin downloading the list of newsgroups, and a dialog box will open.

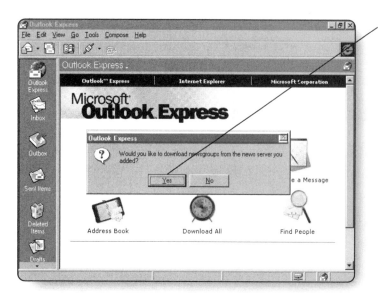

22. **Click** on **Yes**. The list of newsgroups will be transferred to your computer.

SUBSCRIBING TO NEWSGROUPS

To make the messages in a newsgroup easy to view and readily available, you can subscribe to the newsgroup. Now that you have the list of newsgroups that are available from your news server, you can begin the process of selecting one or many in which you have an interest, and you can subscribe to them.

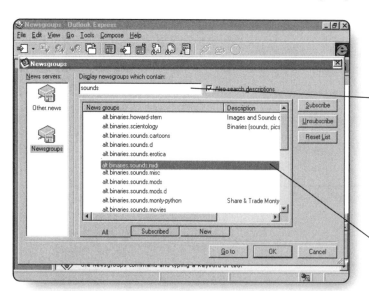

1. **Type** a **keyword** in the Display newsgroups which contain: text box that describes the type of newsgroups that interest you. Newsgroups with matching words will appear in the Newsgroups list.

2. **Click** on the **newsgroup** to which you want to subscribe. The newsgroup will be selected.

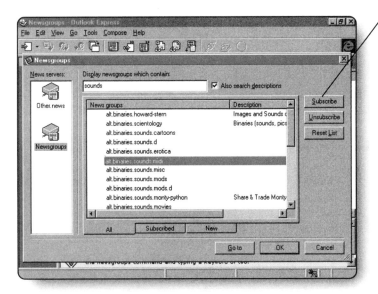

3. **Click** on **Subscribe**. An icon will appear next to the newsgroup name indicating that you have subscribed to this newsgroup.

READING MESSAGES

To read the messages in the groups to which you have subscribed, just follow these steps.

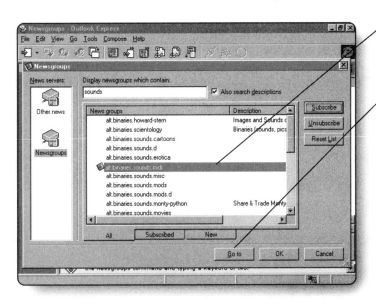

1. **Click** on the **name** of the subscribed newsgroup. The name will be selected.

2. **Click** on **Go to**. The newsgroup headers will start downloading to your computer.

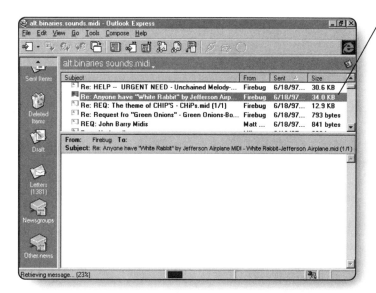

3. **Click** on the **newsgroup message** that you want to read. The message will appear in the preview pane.

NOTE

Newsgroup messages contain text and attachments. Attachments are indicated by a paper clip to the right of the header information.

4. **Cick** on **File**. The File menu will appear.

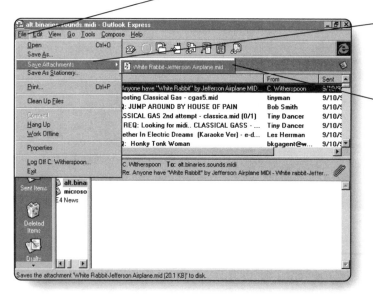

5. **Click** on **Save Attachments**. The list of files attached to the message will appear.

6. **Click** on the attached file that you want to save. The Save Attachment As dialog box will open.

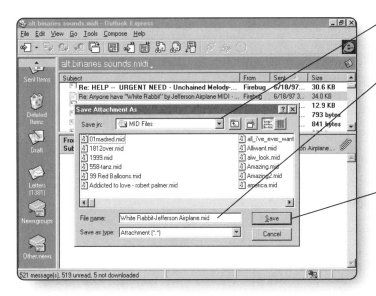

7. **Locate** the **folder** in which you want to save the file.

8. **Type** a **filename** if the filename is not automatically entered in the File name: text box, or if you wish to give it a different filename.

9. **Click** on **Save**. The attachment will be saved to the location that you specified.

POSTING MESSAGES

Sometimes, you will want to post replies to messages posted by others. These could be messages that might be read by the other group members, or messages with attachments that you want to send to the group.

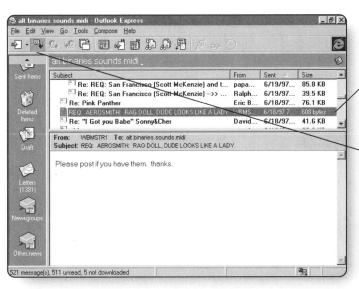

1. **Click** on the **message** to which you want to respond. The message will be selected.

2. **Click** on the **Reply to Group button**. A message window will appear with the newsgroup and subject fields filled in and the original message in the message pane.

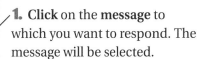

3. **Type** a **reply message** in the message area.

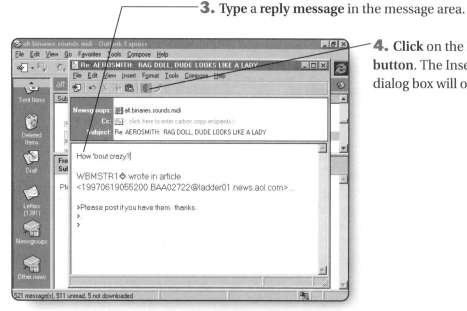

4. **Click** on the **Insert File button**. The Insert Attachment dialog box will open.

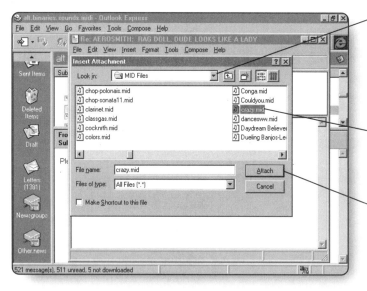

5. **Click** on the **down arrow** (▼) next to the Look in: list box. A drop-down list will appear. **Locate** the **folder** that contains the file you want to attach.

6. **Click** on the **file** that you want to attach. The file will be selected.

7. **Click** on **Attach**. An icon that represents the attached file will appear at the bottom of the message window.

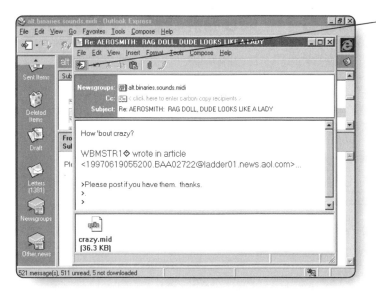

8. Click on the **Post Message button**. The message will be placed in your outbox, and a Post News dialog box will open.

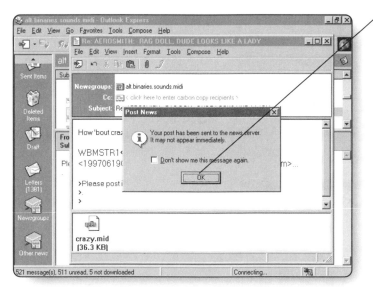

9. Click on **OK**. Your message will be sent to the newsgroup for posting.

USING NEWSGROUP FILTERS

Tons of messages are posted daily to newsgroups. For this reason, you need to be able to separate just the ones that interest you. You can easily set criteria for filtering your newsgroups so that you can exclude the messages that you don't want to view.

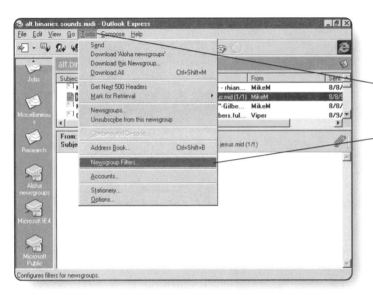

1. Click on Tools. The Tools menu will appear.

2. Click on Newsgroup Filters. The Group Filters dialog box will open.

3. Click on Add. The Filter Properties dialog box will open.

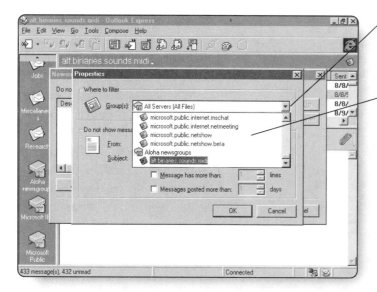

4. **Click** on the **down arrow** (▼) next to the Group(s): list box. A drop-down list will appear.

5. **Click** on a **newsgroup** to filter from the drop-down list. The newsgroup will be selected.

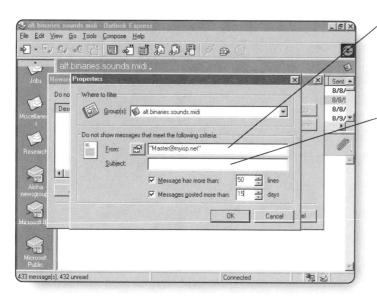

6. **Type** the **e-mail address** in the From: text box that originates messages that you do not want to view.

7. **Type** the **subject line** in the Subject: text box that appears in messages that you do not want to view.

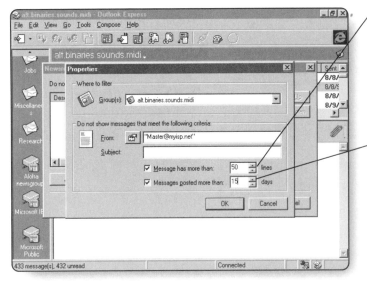

8. Click on **Message has more than:**, and then **click** on the **up and down arrows** (◆) to select a size of messages that you do not want to view if they are more than a certain number of lines.

9. Click on **Messages posted more than:**, and then **click** on the **up and down arrows** (◆) to select the number of days after which a message has become too old for you to view messages.

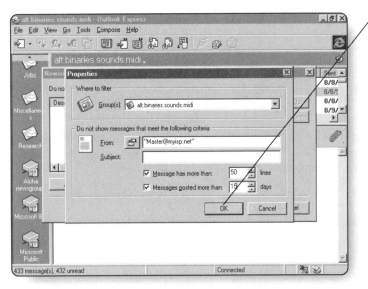

10. Click on **OK**. The Group Filters dialog box will open with the filter listed in the Description field.

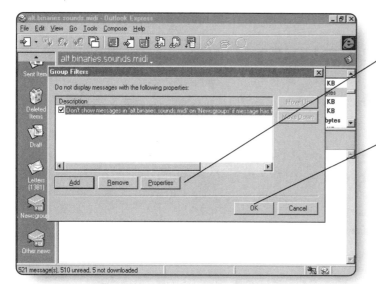

11. Click on OK. The filter will be applied and the types of messages you don't want to view will be blocked from downloading to your computer.

PART III REVIEW QUESTIONS

1. How can you make managing your e-mail easier? *See "Creating a New Folder" in Chapter 9.*

2. What is an easy way to search through a long list of messages to find the message that you need? *See "Finding Messages" in Chapter 9.*

3. What are the three methods you can use to send an e-mail message? *See "Sending Messages" in Chapter 10.*

4. What types of files can be sent as attachments? *See "Sending Attachments" in Chapter 10.*

5. How do you format your e-mail messages so that they look like Web pages? *See "Formatting Your Message" in Chapter 10.*

6. Can you put more than one e-mail address for someone in a single Address Book entry? *See "Adding Contacts to the Address Book" in Chapter 11.*

7. If you routinely send a single e-mail message to a number of people, how can you make this process easier? *See "Forming a Group" in Chapter 11.*

8. How do you add a second newsgroup server to Outlook Express? *See "Setting up a News Account" in Chapter 12.*

9. Why would you want to subscribe to a newsgroup, and how would you do it? *See "Subscribing to Newsgroups" in Chapter 12.*

10. How can you set up Outlook Express to ignore messages that you don't want to see? *See "Using Newsgroup Filters" in Chapter 12.*

PART IV

Keeping in Touch with Microsoft Chat

ush technology" i
own—but what ex
how Microsoft Inter
push technology to
new channels that

13 What's on the Microsoft Chat Screen

This chapter takes you on another visual tour. This visual tour will give you a quick start to using Microsoft Chat. If you enjoy visiting chat rooms, Microsoft Chat can make your visits more enjoyable. Microsoft Chat uses comic book characters that can add animation and expression to your discussions. In this chapter, you'll learn how to:

✦ Configure Microsoft Chat options

✦ Find chat rooms

✦ Find other chat members

✦ Animate a comic character

WORKING WITH MICROSOFT CHAT MENUS

This section will provide you with a basic understanding of the menu commands that are unique to Microsoft Chat.

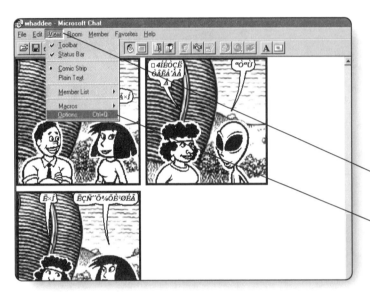

Setting Chat Options

If you want to customize the way you work with Microsoft Chat, you can do this from one convenient place.

1. **Click** on **View**. The View menu will appear.

2. **Click** on **Options**. The Microsoft Chat Options dialog box will open with the Personal Info tab displayed.

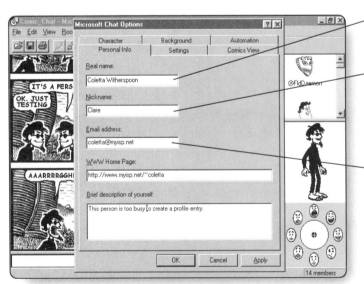

3. **Type** your **name** in the Real name: text box.

4. **Type** the **name** in the Nickname: text box that you want to use while you are in a chat room.

5. **Type** your **e-mail address** in the Email address: text box (this step is optional).

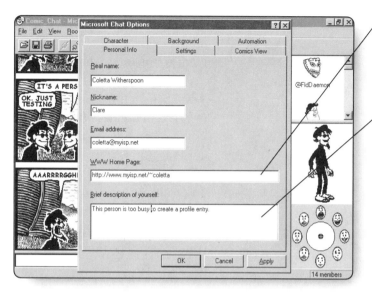

6. Type the **URL** of your personal Web page in the WWW Home Page: text box (this step is optional).

7. Type information about yourself in the Brief description of yourself: text box that you want others to be able to read.

8. Click on the **Settings tab**. The Settings tab will come to the top of the stack.

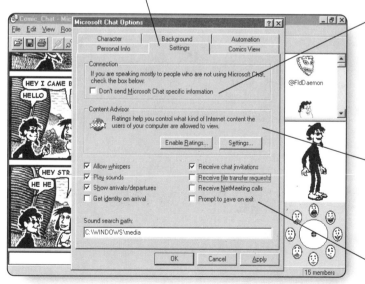

9. Click on **Don't send Microsoft Chat specific information** if you want to disable the comic chat feature. A ✔ will appear in the box.

NOTE

See Chapter 5, "Surfing the Web," for information on setting Content Advisor ratings.

10. Click on any **features** that you want to enable. A ✔ will appear in the boxes of those features that you selected.

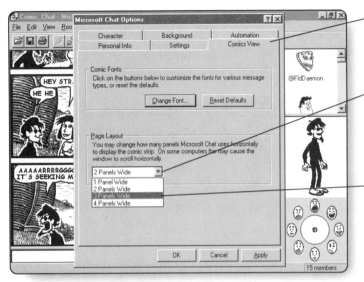

11. **Click** on the **Comics View tab**. The Comics View tab will come to the top of the stack.

12. **Click** on the **down arrow** (▼) next to the Page Layout list box. A drop-down list will appear.

13. **Click** on the **number** of comic strip panels that you want to display horizontally across your screen. The number will be selected.

TIP

Most people will find that three comic strip panels work well.

14. **Click** on the **Character tab**. The Character tab will come to the top of the stack.

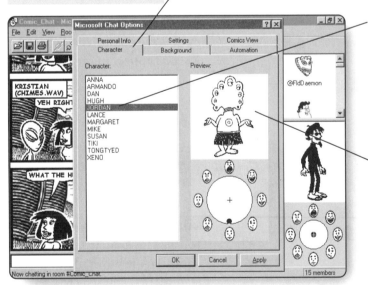

15. **Click** on the **character** in the Character: box that you want to represent you in the chat session. The character will be selected.

TIP

Look in the Preview: pane to see what a character looks like.

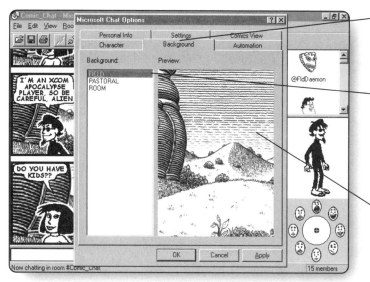

16. **Click** on the **Background tab**. The Background tab will come to the top of the stack.

17. **Click** on the **background** that you want to use for the comic strip. The background will be selected.

TIP

Look in the Preview: pane to see what a background looks like.

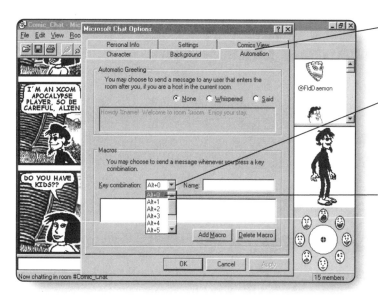

18. **Click** on the **Automation tab**. The Automation tab will come to the top of the stack.

19. **Click** on the **down arrow** (▼) next to the Key combination: list box. A drop-down list will appear.

20. **Click** on the **shortcut key** that you will use when you want to use this macro. The shortcut key will be selected.

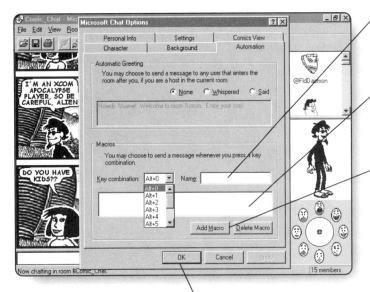

21. Type a **short, descriptive name** for the macro in the Name: text box.

22. Type the **message** in the text box that you want to display when you use the macro.

23. Click on **Add Macro**. The macro will be created and you will be able to use this shortcut any time during a chat session, and the associated message will appear in the chat panel.

24. Click on **OK**. The option settings will be applied.

Finding a Chat Room

Thousands of chat rooms that cover almost every subject are available to choose from. The vast number can almost be overwhelming. Luckily, there is a way to sort through the lists of chat rooms and find one that you will enjoy spending time in.

1. Click on **Room**. The Room menu will appear.

2. Click on **Room List**. The Chat Room List dialog box will open.

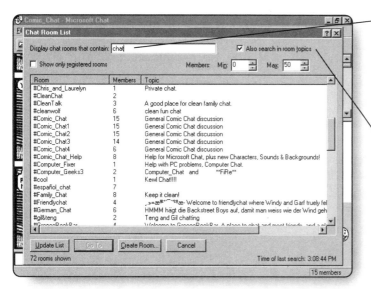

3. Type a **word** in the Display chat rooms that contain: text box that describes the type of chat room discussion you are looking for.

4. Click on **Also search in room topics** to also search the room descriptions for your search word. A ✔ will appear in the box.

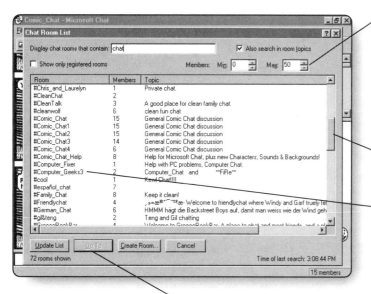

5. Click repeatedly on the **up and down arrows** (◆) next to the Min: and Max: boxes to set the minimum and maximum number of people with whom you want to be in the room.

6. Use the **scroll bar** to look through the list of chat rooms.

7. Click on the **room** that you want to visit. The room listing will be selected.

8. Click on **Go To**. The selected chat discussion will appear in the chat window and you can join the discussion.

Inviting Others to Join a Chat

As you go chatting around, you will meet people with whom you enjoy talking. Sometimes, you may be in a chat room, having a great conversation and you want to invite someone you met previously. Here's how you can find someone and invite that person to join a chat discussion.

1. **Click** on **Member**. The Member menu will appear.

2. **Click** on **User List**. The User List dialog box will open.

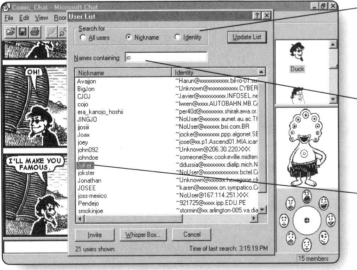

3. **Click** on the **option button** that corresponds to the type of search you want to perform. The option will be selected.

4. **Type** the **name** or **nickname** in the Names containing: text box of the person you are looking for.

5. **Click** on the **name** of the person that matches your search. The name will be selected.

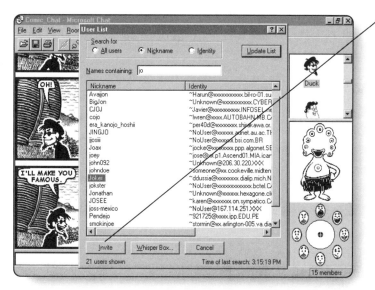

6. **Click** on **Invite**. A message will be sent to that person asking whether he or she wants to join the discussion of the room you are currently in.

Getting Personal Information

Some people make personal information about themselves available to anyone who wants to look for it. Here's a sample of what you can find out about a person.

1. **Click** on the **person** who you want to find out more about. The person's icon will be selected.

2. **Click** on **Member**. The Member menu will appear.

3. **Click** on **Get Profile**. The person's profile will appear in a comic strip panel along with his or her comic character.

4. **Click** on **Member**. The Member menu will appear.

5. **Click** on **Get Identity**. The person's e-mail address will appear in a comic strip panel along with his or her comic character.

LEARNING ABOUT CHAT'S TOOLBARS

Microsoft Chat uses only a few of the toolbar buttons that you see in most Internet Explorer programs. Most of the chat toolbar buttons are unique to Microsoft Chat. Here's a quick tour of the buttons that you may use frequently.

Saving Your Chat Session

When you save a chat session, it is saved in Microsoft's comic chat format. These saved files can be opened only in Microsoft Chat. Not only is the text of the chat session saved, but the comic strip panels are saved as well.

1. **Click** on the **Save button**. The Save As dialog box will open.

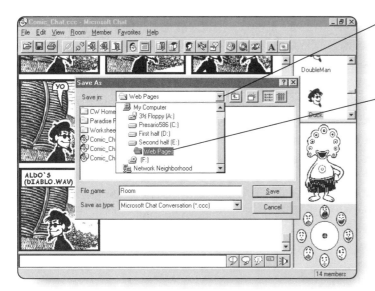

2. **Click** on the **down arrow (▼)** next to the Save in: list box. A drop-down list will appear.

3. **Click** on the **folder** in which you want to save the chat transcript. The folder will be selected.

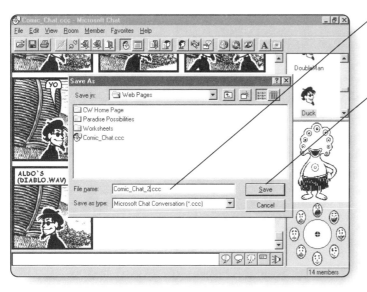

4. **Type** a **filename** for the chat transcript in the File name: text box.

5. **Click** on **Save**. The chat session will be saved and you will be able to view it at another time.

Entering and Exiting Rooms

You may have a couple of rooms that are your favorite places to chat. You can switch among different chat rooms.

1. Click on the **Enter Room button**. The Enter Room dialog box will open.

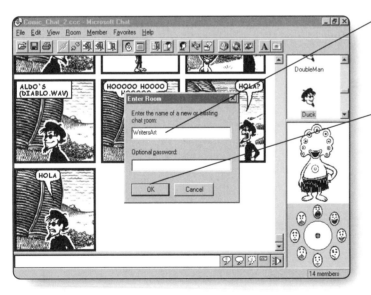

2. Type the **name** of the room that you want to go to in the Enter the name of a new or existing chat room: text box.

3. Click on **OK**. You will join the chat discussion of the room you requested.

4. **Click** on the **Leave Room button** when you want to leave a room. You will be disconnected from the chat server.

Sending E-mail to Chat Members

If you want to correspond privately with someone you met in a chat room, you can try to send the person an e-mail message. This works only if the person chose to make his or her e-mail address public.

1. **Click** on the **member** to whom you want to send an e-mail message. The member's icon will be selected.

2. **Click** on the **E-mail button**. Microsoft Chat will determine whether the person has supplied an e-mail address.

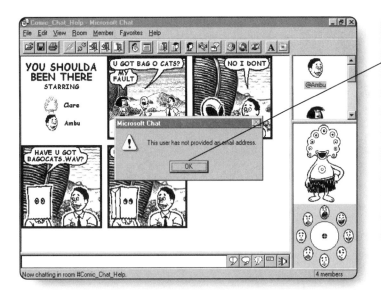

NOTE

If the person has not supplied an e-mail address, a dialog box will open. Click on OK. If the person has provided an e-mail address, a new e-mail message window will appear with the person's e-mail address already entered in the To: area.

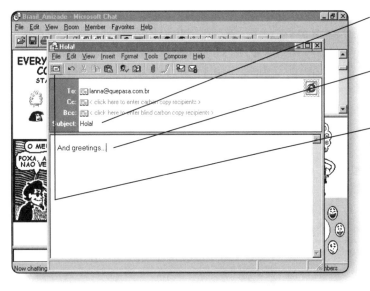

3. Type a **subject** for your message in the Subject: area.

4. Type your **message** in the message area.

5. **Click** on the **Send button**. Your e-mail message will be sent to the recipient.

Setting the Display Font

If you don't like the MS Comic Chat font that displays in the comic strip panels, you can change it to something you like better.

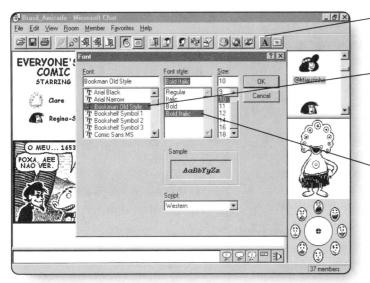

1. **Click** on the **Font button**. The Font dialog box will open.

2. **Click** on the **font** in the Font: list that you want used in the comic strip panels. The font will be selected.

3. **Click** on the **font style** in the Font style: list that you want used in the comic strip panels. The font style will be selected.

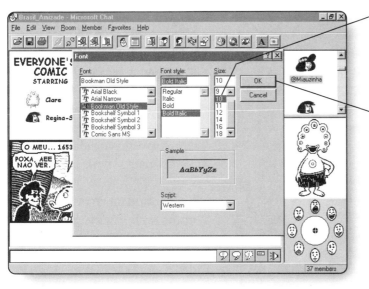

4. **Click** on the **font size** in the Size: list that you want used in the comic strip panels. The font size will be selected.

5. **Click** on **OK**. The new font will appear in the comic strip panel bubbles.

TAKING A LOOK AT MS CHAT'S SCREEN ELEMENTS

The chat window is where you will be doing most of your work in Microsoft Chat. Take a few minutes to learn your way around the screen.

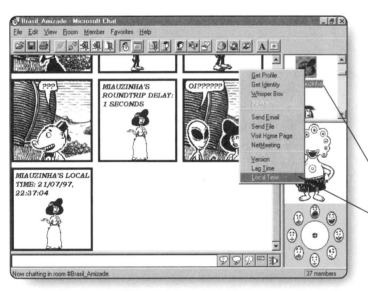

Using the Member List

You can find out a few things about the people with whom you are chatting. Just take a quick look.

1. **Right-click** on a **member's icon**. A menu will appear.

2. **Click** on **Local Time**. A comic strip panel will appear that displays the member's local time.

Changing Your Character's Expression

Each character is capable of eight expressions, and some expressions have different degrees of emotion.

1. **Click** and **hold** your mouse button on the black dot inside the Expression Wheel.

2. Drag the **black dot** toward the different expressions around the wheel. The character in the preview pane will change expressions.

3. Release the **mouse button** on the expression that you want to use. The expression will be applied.

Typing Text

Text is the major element in a chat discussion that keeps the conversation flowing. Not only can you use words to convey your ideas but also special elements to give expression to your text.

1. Type your **message** in the text box at the bottom of the screen.

2. Click on the **Talk button**. Your message will appear in a conversation bubble.

3. Type a **thought** in the text box at the bottom of the screen.

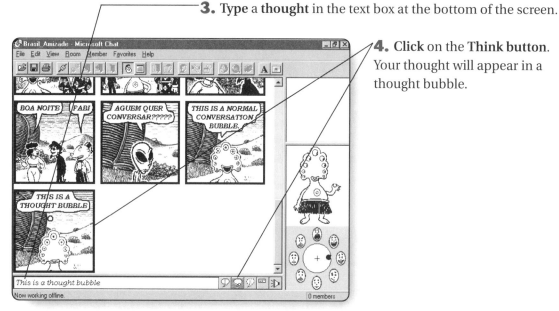

4. **Click** on the **Think button**. Your thought will appear in a thought bubble.

5. Type an **action** in the text box at the bottom of the screen.

6. **Click** on the **Action button**. Your name will appear before the thought in an action box.

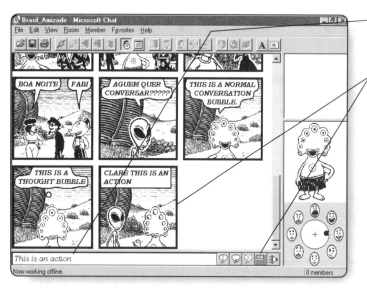

14 Participating in a Chat Group

Participating in a chat room discussion has been a mainstay activity of Internet users since the beginning. It is a great way to get together with a group of people with similar interests and discuss almost anything. This chapter will give you a good introduction to chat and lead you through the business of setting yourself up and joining a discussion group. In this chapter, you'll learn how to:

✦ Select a chat server

✦ Select a character

✦ Join a chat discussion

✦ Meet other members

✦ Save your chat session

FINDING A CHAT SERVER

Chat is a fun way to communicate with people on the Net, and there are several ways to connect with someone for a chat conversation. One of these is to connect with an ILS server. In the following section, you will select a chat server and then a chat room with a topic that interests you, and you will learn about how to join in the conversation.

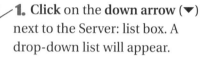

1. Click on the **down arrow** (▼) next to the Server: list box. A drop-down list will appear.

2. Click on a **chat server**. The chat server will be selected.

3. Click on the **option button** to show all chat rooms available on the chat server. The option will be selected.

4. Click on **OK**. The Chat Room List dialog box will open.

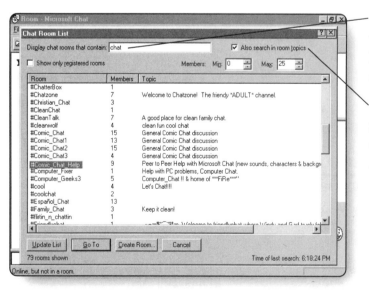

5. Type a **word** that describes the chat discussion you would like to join. This will narrow down the list of chat rooms.

6. Click on **Also search in room topics** to search the topic column for your search word. A ✔ will appear in the box.

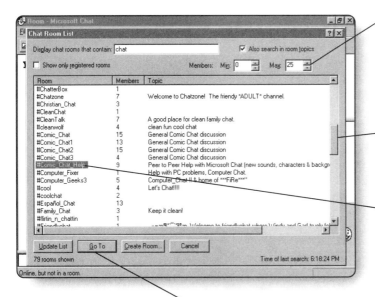

7. Click on the **up and down arrows** (♦) to choose the number of people you want to see in a chat room. The number of people will be selected.

8. **Scroll through** the list of chat rooms that meet your search criteria.

9. Click on the **chat room** that you would like to join. The chat room will be selected.

10. Click on **Go To**. The selected room will appear in the chat window.

NOTE

You can start reading the chat discussion in progress.

JOINING THE DISCUSSION

Joining in the discussion is probably what you came here for, so now you need to see what kinds of things are available to help you make that happen.

Ask Questions First

After you read some of the comments in the discussion, you may want to take part. There is help available to members of some moderated chat rooms, and here's how to find it.

1. Read the **chat panels** to see whether any type of automated help is available.

2. Type the **commands** for help and **press** the **Enter key**. The request will display.

3. Read the **chat room rules** and follow them. Failure to follow the rules will get you kicked out of a room.

Speaking Up

Someone has just said something that you want to comment on. The following steps show you how to send the comment.

1. Click on the **character** to which you want to respond. The character will be selected.

2. Press and **hold** the **mouse button** on the black dot and **drag** it around to set the expression for your character. The character's expression will appear in the preview pane.

3. Release the **mouse button** on the desired expression. The expression will be selected.

4. Type your **message** in the text box.

5. Click on the **Talk button**. Your message will appear.

NOTE

When you type a long message, it will appear in several panels.

Playing Sounds

You can also enhance the chat experience with the addition of sounds. You can play a sound to accompany what your character is saying.

1. **Select** an **expression** for your character (see the previous section, "Speaking Up," if you don't remember how to do this).

2. **Click** on the **Sound button**. The Play Sound dialog box will open.

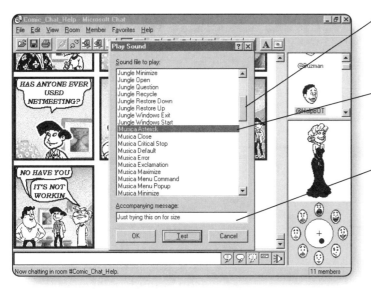

3. Drag the **scroll bar** until you see the sound that you want to play.

4. Click on the **sound**. The name of the sound will be selected.

5. Type a **message** to display in a panel to accompany the sound.

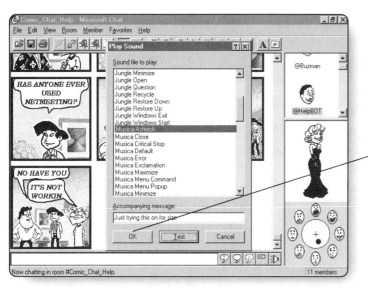

TIP

If you want to listen to a sound before you send your message, click on the Test button.

6. Click on **OK**. The message will appear and the sound will play.

MEETING OTHER MEMBERS

Meeting other members of the chat conversation is really simple. You can look at their profiles by clicking on their icon and following menu choices. You can also get a member's identity in the same way.

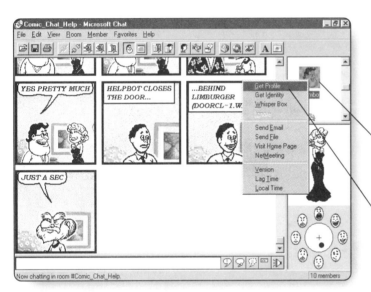

Getting a Profile

Getting the profile for another member of the chat session is easy.

1. **Right-click** on the **person's icon**. A shortcut menu will appear.

2. **Click** on **Get Profile**.

The person's profile will appear in a separate panel.

Getting an Identity

Follow the same sort of process as "Getting a Profile" to get an identification for the other member.

1. **Right-click** on the **person's icon**. A shortcut menu will appear.

2. Click on **Get Identity**.

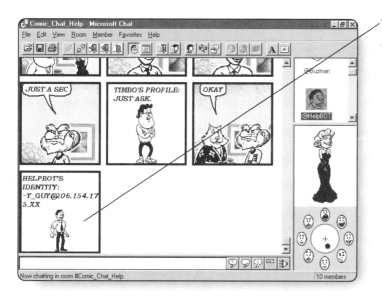

The person's e-mail address will appear in a separate panel.

Finding Another Member's Time Zone

It helps to put things in perspective if you have an idea of what time it is for the person with whom you are chatting.

1. **Right-click** on the **person's icon**. A shortcut menu will appear.

2. **Click** on Local Time.

The person's local time will appear in a separate panel.

SAVING YOUR CHAT SESSION

Sometimes, you may wish to save a particularly interesting or important chat discussion.

1. **Click** on the **Save button**. The Save As dialog box will open.

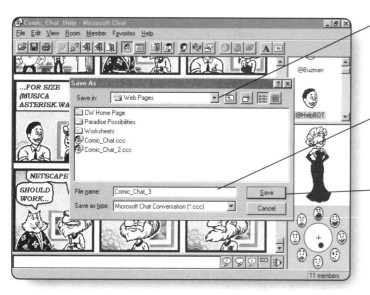

2. **Click** on the **drive** and **folder** to contain the saved chat session. The drive and folder will be selected.

3. **Type** a **name** for the chat session in the File name: text box.

4. **Click** on **Save**. The chat session will be saved to the file you specified.

USING URL ADDRESSES DURING A CHAT SESSION

URL addresses are available for your use during a chat session. You may display them for other chat members to see and you may use them to access Web pages.

Displaying a URL Address

You can display a URL as information for other chat members or as a link so that they might go there.

1. Select an expression for your character (see "Speaking Up" in this chapter if you don't remember how to do this).

2. Type a URL address.

3. Press the Enter key. The URL address will appear in blue text in a panel.

Accessing Web Pages

You may use the URL address that appears in the chat panel to access Web pages.

1. **Double-click** on the **URL address**.

The Web page associated with the URL address will appear in an Internet Explorer window.

FINDING MORE CHARACTERS

If you are not completely satisfied with the choices for characters, backgrounds, and sounds that you have, you can get more characters from Microsoft and other places.

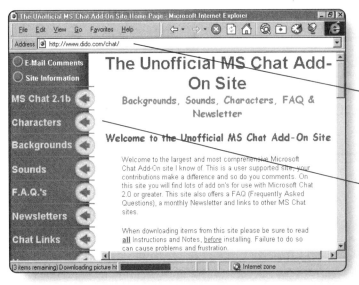

1. Open Internet Explorer.

2. Type **www.dido.com/chat/** in the Address Bar. The Unofficial Microsoft Chat Add-On Site Home Page will appear.

3. Click on the **type** of add-on that you want to install, and read the directions at the Web site.

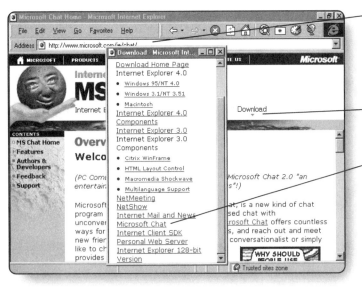

4. Type **www.microsoft.com/ ie/chat/** in the Address Bar. The Microsoft Chat Home page will appear.

5. Click on the **Download link**. A menu will appear.

6. Click on **Microsoft Chat**. The Internet Explorer Products Download page will appear.

7. **Scroll down** the page to the section where you choose the version of Microsoft Chat you want to install.

8. **Click** on the **down arrow** (▼). A drop-down list of options will appear.

9. **Click** on **Additional Chat Characters Pack**. This selection will display in the list box.

10. **Click** on **Next**. Another Web page will appear that lists the available download sites. Read the directions before downloading the character pack.

PART IV REVIEW QUESTIONS

1. How do you change the comic character that represents you? *See "Setting Chat Options" in Chapter 13.*

2. How do you narrow down the list of chat rooms in a server so that you can more easily find the room you want to join? *See "Finding a Chat Room" in Chapter 13.*

3. How do you invite your friends to visit with you in a particular chat room? *See "Inviting Others to Join a Chat" in Chapter 13.*

4. What information can you find about the other people you are chatting with in a chat room? *See "Getting Personal Information" in Chapter 13.*

5. How can you move from chat room to chat room? *See "Entering and Exiting Rooms" in Chapter 13.*

6. How do you ask for general help in a moderated chat room? *See "Ask Questions First" in Chapter 14.*

7. How do you change the expression on your chat character's face? *See "Speaking Up" in Chapter 14.*

8. How do you add sound to a chat discussion? *See "Playing Sounds" in Chapter 14.*

9. Where do you look to find the e-mail address of someone in a chat room? *See "Getting an Identity" in Chapter 14.*

10. How do you create a hyperlink in your chat message so that other people in the chat room can click on it and access the specified Web page? *See "Displaying a URL Address" in Chapter 14.*

PART V

Virtual Conferencing with NetMeeting

gazine

UPPORT

plore

eb

f the wee

pecial De
Bringing Yo

ush technology" is
own—but what exa
how Microsoft Inter
push technology to
new channels that

15 What's on the NetMeeting Screen

Feeling comfortable with your environment, especially when talking with someone, is essential to good communication. Being in a familiar environment and feeling that you are in control will always make things work much more smoothly. All you need to do to gain that feeling of familiarity and control is to learn your way around the NetMeeting screen and become familiar with the screen elements and the choices and options available to you. In this chapter, you'll learn how to:

✦ **Use NetMeeting's menus**

✦ **Work with the toolbars**

✦ **Take advantage of NetMeeting's screen elements**

NAVIGATING THROUGH NETMEETING'S MENUS

The menus on the NetMeeting screen contain all of the options and actions available to you in the NetMeeting program. You can use the menu selections to set NetMeeting options and to block incoming calls.

NOTE

If this is the first time that you are using NetMeeting, a setup wizard will start that will walk you through the process of getting NetMeeting ready to use. The wizard will ask you for your name, e-mail address, a directory server that you want to use, and information about your computer. The wizard will also tune your computer's sound settings so that you can send and receive voice transmissions.

Blocking Incoming Calls

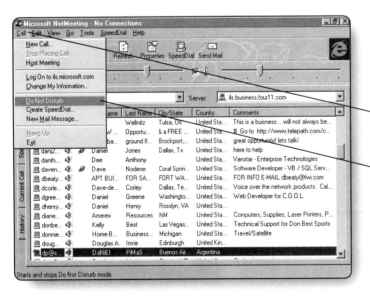

NetMeeting has a way for you to ensure that you are not disturbed by incoming calls if you don't want to be.

1. Click on **Call**. The Call menu will appear.

2. Click on **Do Not Disturb**. A dialog box will open.

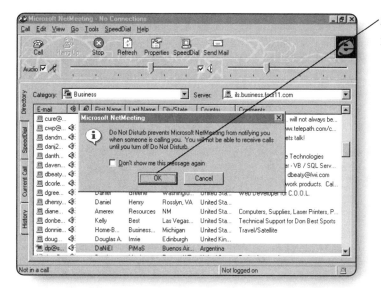

3. **Click** on **OK**. NetMeeting will not answer incoming calls.

4. **Click** on **Call**. The Call menu will appear.

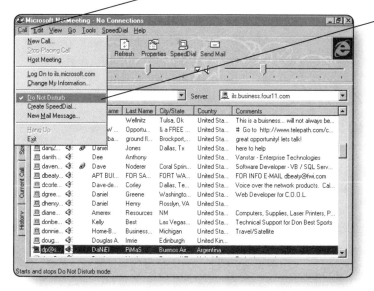

5. **Click** on **Do Not Disturb**. NetMeeting will go back to answering incoming calls.

Finding More ILS Listings

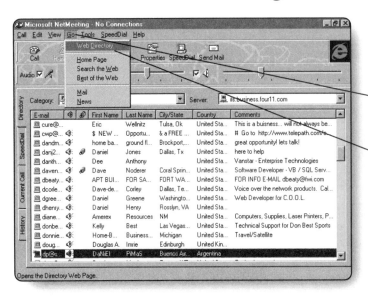

You may want to find other servers that have other NetMeeting participants.

1. **Click** on **Go**. The Go menu will appear.

2. **Click** on **Web Directory**. The NetMeeting Search Web page will appear.

3. **Browse** the **Web site**. You will find ILS servers, a way to search for people, and information about NetMeeting.

Setting NetMeeting Options

Using menu commands makes it simple to set NetMeeting's options to make sure that you have everything the way you want it when NetMeeting is open.

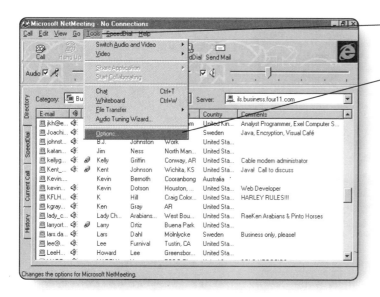

1. **Click** on **Tools**. The Tools menu will appear.

2. **Click** on **Options**. The Options dialog box will open.

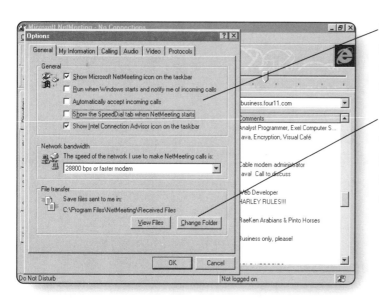

3. **Click** on **items** that you want to enable when NetMeeting is open. A ✔ will appear next to those you selected.

4. **Click** on **Change Folder**. You will be able to change the folder where files that are transferred to you during a conference are stored.

5. **Click** on the **My Information tab**. The My Information tab will come to the top of the stack.

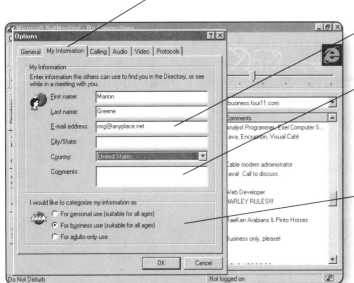

6. **Type** any **changes** to your personal information as needed.

7. **Type information** in the Comments: text box that you want to appear in the Comments column of your ILS directory listing.

8. **Click** on the **option button** for the category under which you want to be listed in the ILS directory. The option will be selected.

9. **Click** on the **Calling tab**. The Calling Options tab will come to the top of the stack.

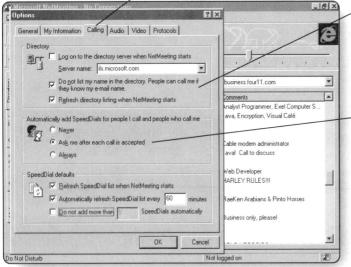

10. **Click** on **Do not list my name in the directory** if you do not want a listing in the ILS directory. A ✔ will appear in the box.

11. **Click** on the **option button** to select how entries are added to the SpeedDial. The option will be selected.

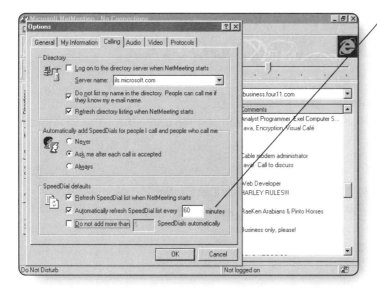

12. **Click** on **Automatically refresh SpeedDial list every** to automatically update your SpeedDial list, and then **type** the **number** of minutes between updates in the text box. A ✔ will appear in the check box and the number of minutes you typed will appear in the blank box.

13. **Click** on the **Audio tab**. The Audio tab will come to the top of the stack.

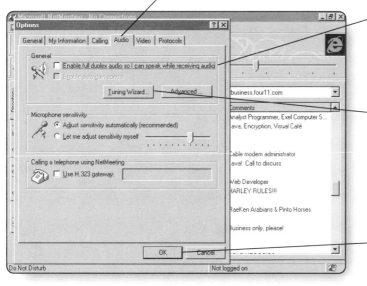

14. **Click** on **Enable full duplex audio** to remove the ✔ to enable half-duplex audio. The ✔ will be removed.

15. **Click** on **Tuning Wizard**. The Tuning Wizard will start and you can adjust your sound settings if you are having problems sending or receiving audio.

16. **Click** on **OK**. Your settings will be applied.

MAKING THINGS EASY WITH TOOLBARS

The toolbar buttons can adjust the speaker volume, display a directory listing's properties, or send a message. They offer easy one-click access to information and controls for audio and video.

Displaying a Directory Listing's Properties

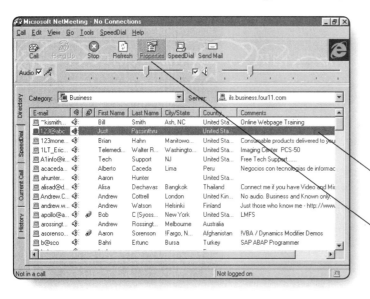

The directory listing's properties sheet contains information such as the name and e-mail address of the person listed along with some auto-detected information about the person's audio/video capabilities.

1. Click on a **directory listing**. The listing will be selected.

2. Click on the **Properties button**. The Properties sheet will appear.

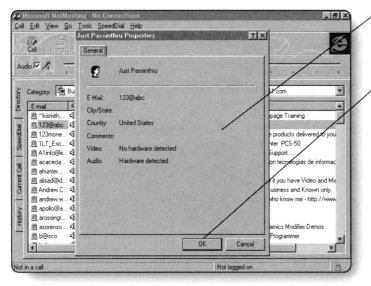

3. **Make** a **note** of the person's e-mail address or hardware configuration.

4. **Click** on **OK**. The Properties sheet will close and the directory list will appear.

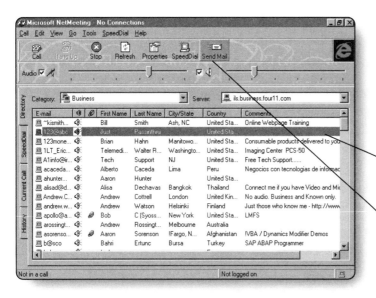

Sending a Message

You can use the toolbar to make sending a message to someone easy.

1. **Click** on a **directory listing**. The listing will be selected.

2. **Click** on the **Send Mail button**. A new message window will appear with the recipient's e-mail address already filled in.

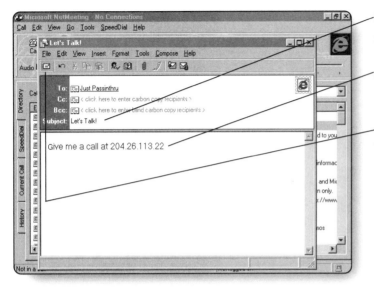

3. Type a **subject** for your message in the Subject: area.

4. Type your **message** in the message area.

5. Click on the **Send button**. Your message will be sent to the recipient.

Adjusting the Volume

You may have to adjust the speaker volume in order to understand the audio portion of your NetMeeting conference.

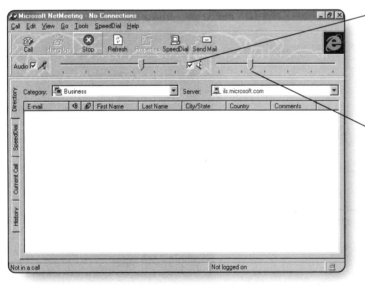

1. Click in the **box** next to the sound icon. A ✔ will appear in the box and you will be able to hear the voice of the person with whom you are conferencing.

2. Press and hold the **mouse button** on the slider bar and **drag** it to increase or decrease your speaker volume.

3. Release the **mouse button** at your desired volume level. The volume level will be selected.

TAKING A LOOK AT NETMEETING'S SCREEN ELEMENTS

The screen elements included with NetMeeting include the frame for displaying the directory listings and the slider bars for the speaker volume control. In the following steps, you will see how to use the screen elements to your best advantage.

Displaying Directory Listings

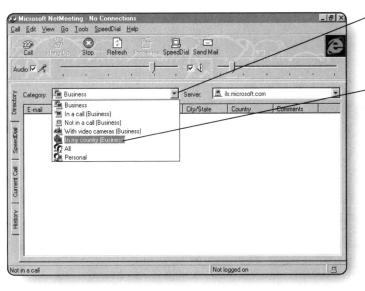

1. **Click** on the **down arrow (▼)** next to the Category: list box. A drop-down list will appear.

2. **Click** on the **type** of **conference call** you want to make. The type will be selected.

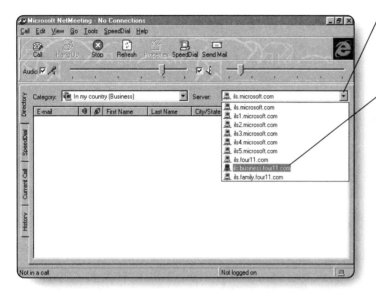

3. **Click** on the **down arrow** (▼) next to the Server: list box. A drop-down list will appear.

4. **Click** on an **ILS server**. The server will be selected.

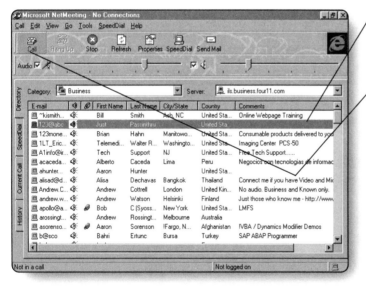

5. **Click** on the **listing** of the person you want to call. The listing will be selected.

6. **Click** on the **Call button**. Your call will be connected if the other person is available and willing to take the call.

Displaying Your Current Call

You can display the status of your current NetMeeting conference call. Included in this information is a list of the other participants in the conference. There are also controls for the audio and video portions of the NetMeeting connection.

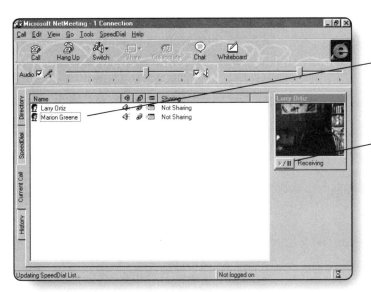

1. Click on the **video control** to start or stop any video transmission. The video will begin playing or stop playing in the Remote Video window.

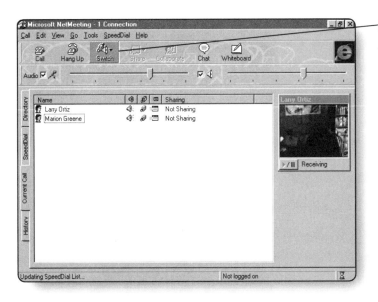

2. Click on the **Switch button**. A menu will appear and you can choose which caller can send video transmissions.

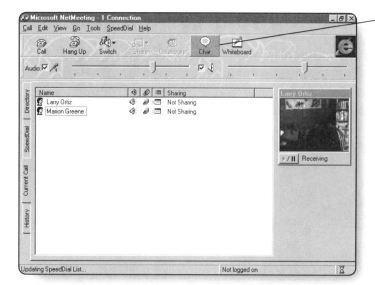

3. **Click** on the **Chat button**. The Chat window will appear.

TIP

There may be times while you are talking to a friend or colleague when you will have problems understanding each others' voices. This is probably caused by transmission delays on the Internet. During these times, use the Chat tool to communicate with each other.

16 Participating in a NetMeeting Conference

Meetings are a part of what makes any business or endeavor run smoothly. With NetMeeting you can have those meetings easily and effectively right at your desk. Today with everything and everyone spread out all over, NetMeeting can save time and facilitate meetings with people who may be widely disbursed. In this chapter, you'll learn how to:

✦ Make a connection to others

✦ Find an ILS server

✦ Use the Chat tool, speed dialer, and Whiteboard

CONNECTING TO OTHERS

Connecting to others is the object here, of course, and there are a couple of ways that you can do it. You can connect through an ILS server or directly over the Internet.

Finding a Net-Meeting Server

The following steps will lead you through the process of finding a NetMeeting server you can use.

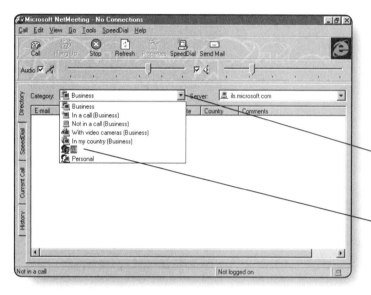

1. **Click** on the **down arrow (▼)** next to the Category: list box. A list of categories will appear.

2. **Click** on the **category** that includes the type of people with whom you want to conference. The category will appear in the Category: list box.

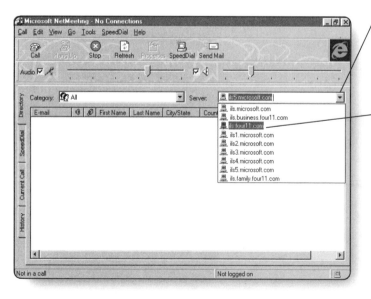

3. **Click** on the **down arrow (▼)** next to the Server: list box. A list of available conference servers will appear.

4. **Click** on the **conference server** that you want to access. The server will appear in the Server: list box, and the directory list for the server will download.

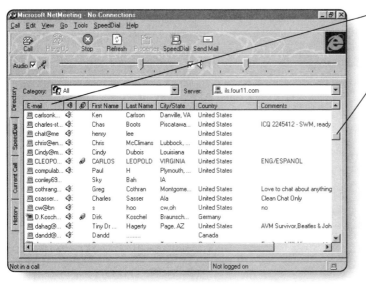

5. Click on the **E-mail column**. The directory list will sort alphabetically by e-mail address.

6. Scroll through the directory listing until you find the person with whom you want to conference.

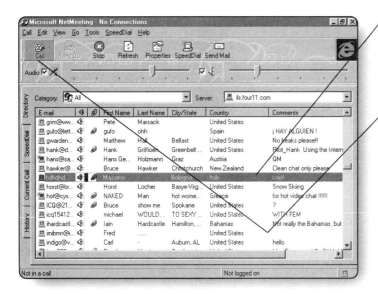

7. Click on the **listing** for the person with whom you want to conference. The listing will be selected.

8. Click on the **Call button**. The New Call dialog box will open.

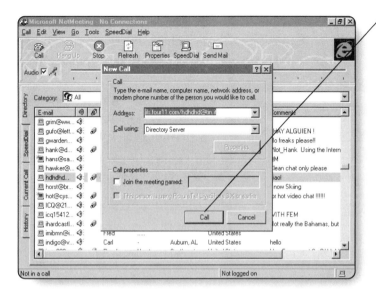

9. **Click** on **Call**. NetMeeting will attempt to connect with the other person.

Connecting through the Internet

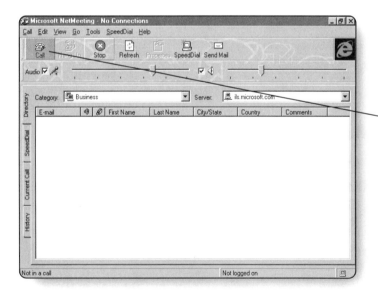

If you know the IP address of the person with whom you wish to conference, you can connect directly over the Internet.

1. **Click** on the **Call button**. The New Call dialog box will open.

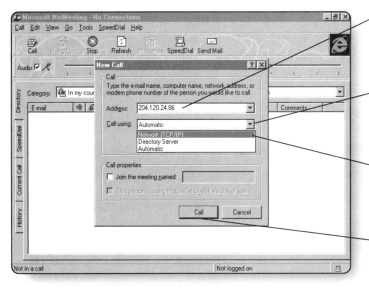

2. Type the **IP Address** in the Address: box of the person with whom you want to conference.

3. Click on the **down arrow** (▼) next to the Call using: list box. A drop-down list will appear.

4. Click on **Network** from the drop-down list. Network will be selected.

5. Click on **Call**. NetMeeting will attempt to call the person with whom you want to conference.

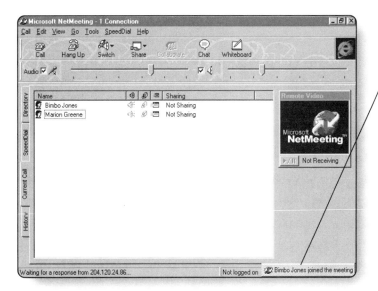

NOTE

When the person has joined the conference, a message will appear at the bottom of your screen and the person's name will be listed in the Current Call window. You are now ready to start your conference.

USING SPEEDDIAL

SpeedDial will help you to keep track of people you want to call and will also allow you to connect to them.

Adding a SpeedDial Entry

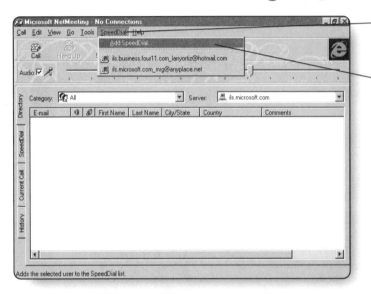

1. Click on **SpeedDial**. The SpeedDial menu will appear.

2. Click on **Add SpeedDial**. The Add SpeedDial dialog box will open.

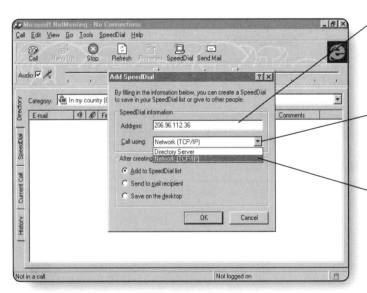

3. Type the **IP Address** in the Address: text box of the person for whom you want to create a SpeedDial listing.

4. Click on the **down arrow** (▼) next to the Call using: list box. A drop-down list will appear.

5. Click on the **type of network connection** needed to connect to that person. The network connection will be selected.

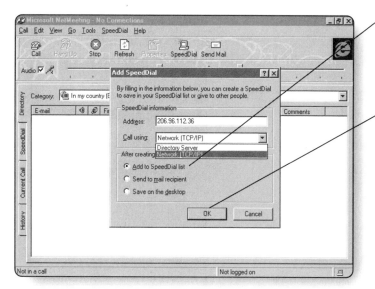

6. **Click** on the **Add to SpeedDial list option** to add this entry to the SpeedDial list. The option will be selected.

7. **Click** on **OK**. A new entry will be created in the SpeedDial list.

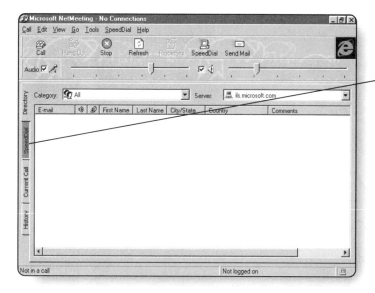

Connecting With the SpeedDial

1. **Click** on the **SpeedDial tab**. The SpeedDial window will appear.

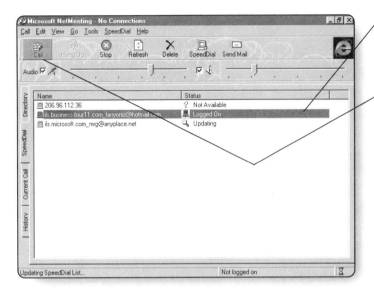

2. **Click** on the **SpeedDial entry** for the person you want to call. The entry will be selected.

3. **Click** on the **Call button**. The New Call dialog box will open.

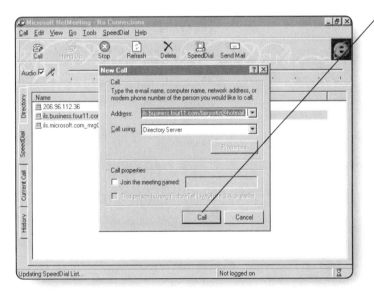

4. **Click** on **Call**. NetMeeting will attempt to connect to the person you are trying to call.

USING CHAT TO HAVE A PRIVATE CONVERSATION

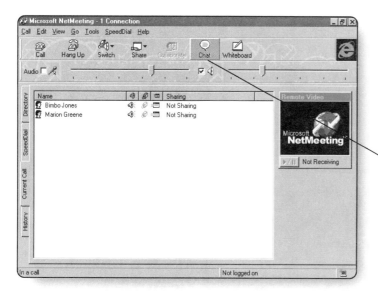

You can use Chat to have a private conversation during a NetMeeting session.

Having a Conversation

1. **Click** on the **Chat button**. The Chat tool will appear.

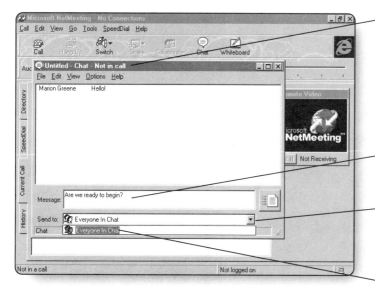

2. **Type** your **message** in the Message: text box.

3. **Click** on the **down arrow** (▼) next to the Send to: list box. A drop-down list will appear.

4. **Click** on which **people** you want to see the message. The people will be selected.

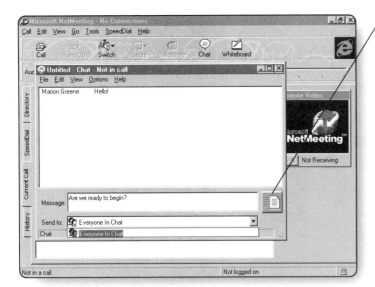

5. **Click** on the **Post button**. Your message will be visible in the chat area.

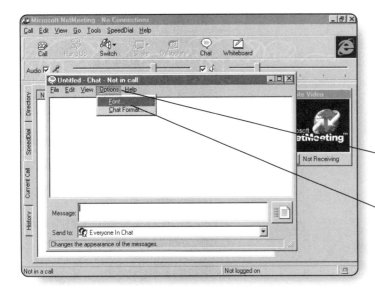

Changing Chat Options

You can easily change the Chat options to suit your needs or wishes.

1. **Click** on **Options**. The Options menu will appear.

2. **Click** on **Font**. The Font dialog box will open.

3. Click on the **font** in the Font: box that you want to use to display the text in the Chat tool window. The font will be selected.

4. Click on the **font style** in the Font style: box that you want to use to display the text in the Chat tool window. The font style will be selected.

5. Click on the **font size** in the Size: box that you want to use to display the text in the Chat tool window. The size will be selected.

6. Click on **OK**. The font that displays in the Chat tool window will change.

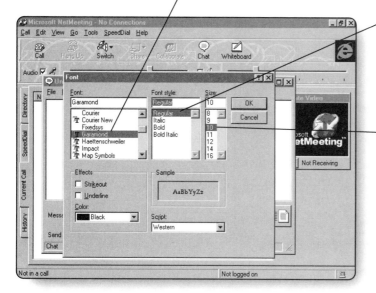

7. Click on **Options**. The Options menu will appear.

8. Click on **Chat Format**. The Chat Format dialog box will open.

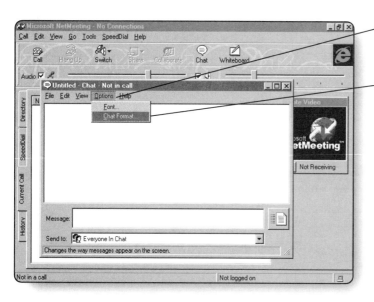

9. Click on those **items** in the Information display area that you want to display in the Chat tool window. A ✔ will appear in the box next to the items you selected.

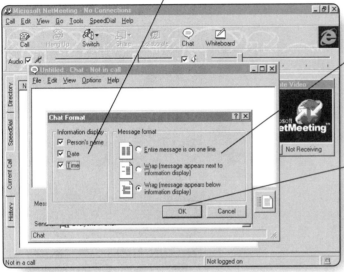

10. Click on the **option button** in the Message format area for the format you want to use to display the messages. The option will be selected.

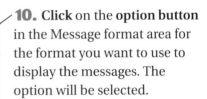

11. Click on **OK**. The format of the Chat tool window will change.

Saving a Conversation

1. Click on **File**. The File menu will appear.

2. Click on **Save**. The Save As dialog box will open.

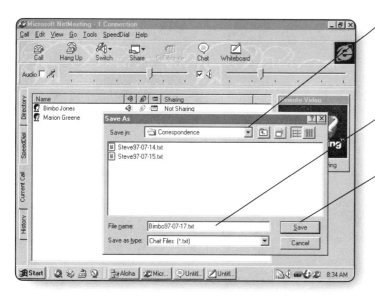

3. **Select** the **folder** where you want to save your Chat conversation. The folder will be selected.

4. **Type** a **name** for the Chat file in the File name: text box.

5. **Click** on **Save**. The chat file will be stored on your computer.

MAKING YOUR POINT WITH THE WHITEBOARD

You can take advantage of the power of the Whiteboard tool in your NetMeeting sessions. You can share ideas and keep track of a meeting on the Whiteboard tool in the same way that a chalkboard is used in a confer-ence room. The NetMeeting Whiteboard tool allows you to add images along with text, offers several ways to highlight information so that it stands out, and lets you save infor-mation to use at a later time.

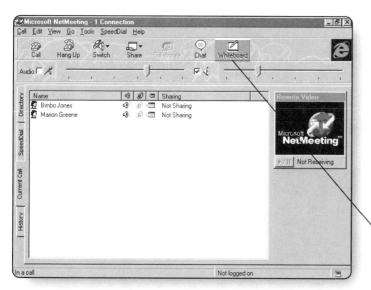

Opening the Whiteboard

1. **Click** on the **Whiteboard button**. The Whiteboard will open.

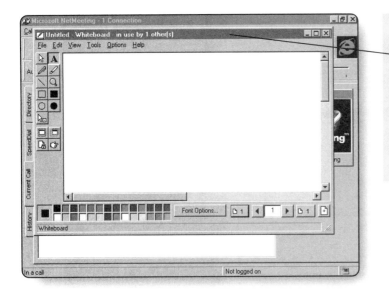

NOTE
You will have to wait until everyone has opened their Whiteboard tool. The title bar will display the number of people who have their copy of the Whiteboard tool open.

Adding Text

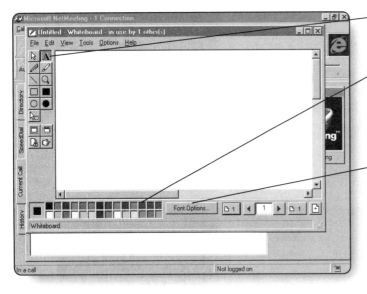

1. **Click** on the **Text Tool button**. The Text Tool will be selected.

2. **Click** on the **color** that you want to use for the text. The color will appear in the selected color box.

3. **Click** on **Font Options**. The Font dialog box will open.

4. **Click** on the **font** in the Font: box that you want to use to display the text in the Chat tool window. The font will be selected.

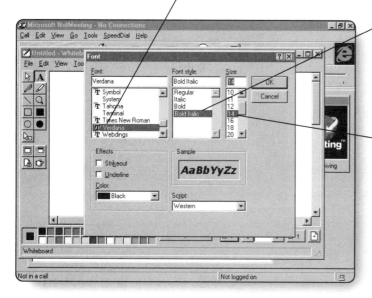

5. **Click** on the **font style** in the Font style: box that you want to use to display the text in the Chat tool window. The font style will be selected.

6. **Click** on the **font size** in the Size: box that you want to use to display the text in the Chat tool window. The size will be selected.

7. **Click** on **OK**. The Whiteboard tool will appear.

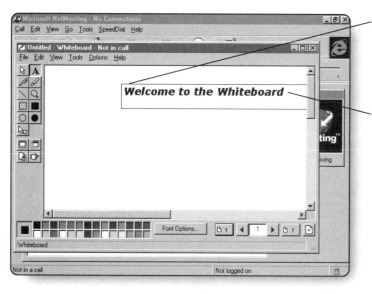

8. **Click** on the **location** where you want to start typing your text. A cursor will appear outlined by a black box.

9. **Type** your **text**.

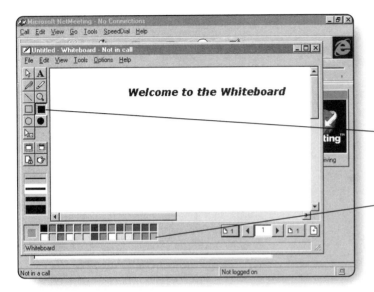

Adding Shapes

You can add shapes to your Whiteboard presentation by selecting them from the toolbar.

1. Click on the **Filled Rectangle tool button**. The Filled Rectangle tool will be selected.

2. Click on the **color** that you want the rectangle to be. The color will appear in the selected color box.

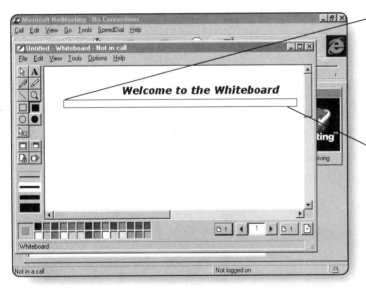

3. Press and hold the mouse button on the location where you want to start the rectangle and drag the mouse pointer to the location where you want to end the rectangle.

4. Release the mouse button. A filled rectangle will appear on the Whiteboard.

Moving Objects

You can move things around on the Whiteboard by using the mouse.

1. **Click** on the **Selector tool button**. The mouse cursor will change to an arrow.

2. **Click** on the **object** that you want to move. A dotted border will appear around the object.

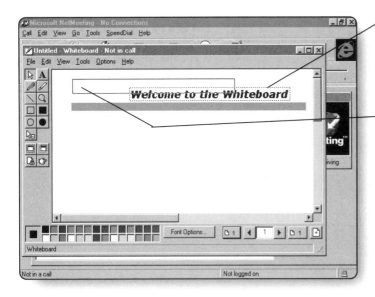

3. Press and **hold** the **mouse button** on the object while you drag it toward the desired position.

4. **Release** the **mouse button** when the object is positioned where you want it. The object will be moved to the new position.

Adding Images to the Whiteboard

Images may be added to your Whiteboard presentation by using the Whiteboard tools.

1. **Display** the **object** that you want to copy onto the Whiteboard.

NOTE

You can copy any object, whether it's on your desktop or accessed from another program, and paste it onto the Whiteboard tool. If you want to copy something from your desktop, mini-mize all open programs. If you want to copy part of a file that is open in another application, make sure no other program windows are overlapping the file you want to copy.

2. Click on the **Whiteboard button**. The Whiteboard tool will appear in front of the object you want to copy.

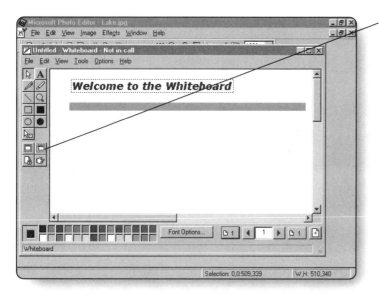

3. Click on the **Copy Selected tool**. The Whiteboard will minimize itself and a dialog box will open.

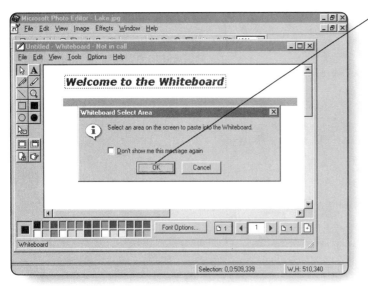

4. **Click** on **OK**. The object that you want to copy will appear.

5. **Press** and **hold** the **mouse button** at the upper-left corner of the area that you want to copy and **drag** the **mouse** to the lower-right corner. A dotted line will appear around the selected area.

6. **Release** the **mouse button**. The selection will be pasted to the upper-left corner of the Whiteboard window.

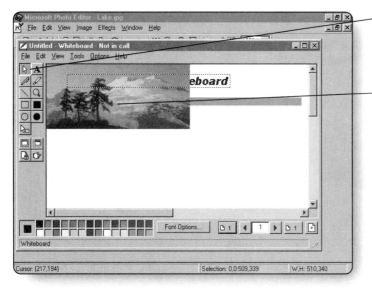

7. **Click** on the **Selector tool button**. The mouse cursor will change to an arrow.

8. **Press** and **hold** the **mouse button** on the object and **drag** the **object** to the desired position.

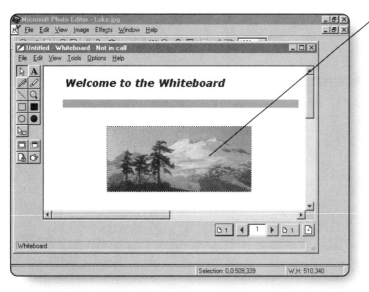

9. **Release** the **mouse button**. The object will move.

Saving the Whiteboard Contents

1. **Click** on **File**. The File menu will appear.

2. **Click** on **Save**. The Save As dialog box will open.

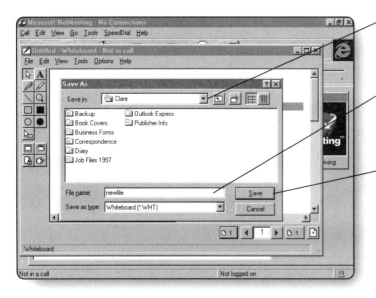

3. **Select** the **folder** where the file is to be saved. The folder will be selected.

4. **Type** a **name** for the Whiteboard file in the File name: text box.

5. **Click** on **Save**. The file will be saved to the selected folder on your computer.

17 Sharing Documents During a Conference

One of the most useful aspects of meetings and conferences is that they provide an opportunity for the people involved to share information with everyone looking at the same documents. With NetMeeting, the group can also share applications, as you will see by following along through this section. In this chapter, you'll learn how to:

✦ Share an application and make changes to a file during a conference

✦ Transfer files to other people in a conference

✦ Receive files from other people in a conference

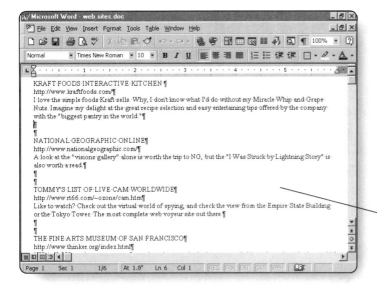

SHARING APPLICATIONS

You can share a Word document across the Net with someone who doesn't have Word, allowing that person to share and work in your Word application, much like telnet.

1. Open the **application** and the **document** that you want to share during the conference.

2. Click on the **NetMeeting icon** on the Windows taskbar. You will switch to the NetMeeting window.

3. Click on **Tools**. The Tools menu will appear.

4. Click on **Share Application**. A cascading menu will appear.

5. Click on the **name** of the application and document that you want to share. A dialog box will open.

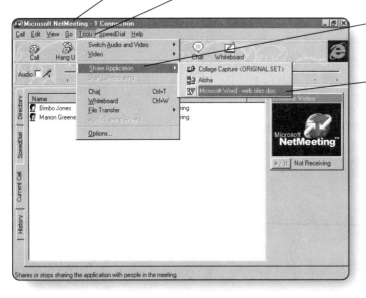

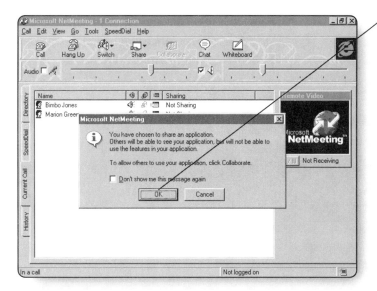

6. **Click** on **OK**. Everyone in the conference will be able to see the document but will not be able to make any changes to it.

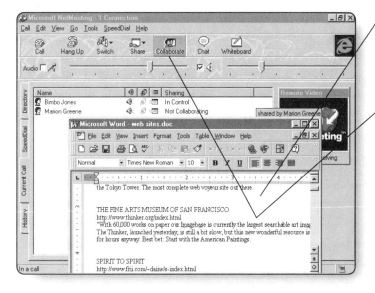

7. **Make** any **changes** to the document as needed. The changes will appear on each person's screen.

8. **Click** on the **Collaborate button**. A dialog box will open.

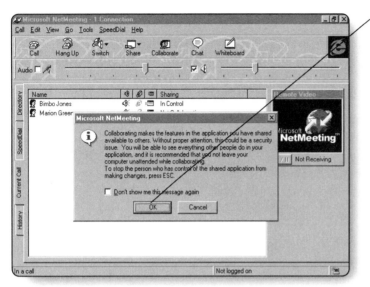

9. **Click** on **OK**. Everyone in the conference will be able to make changes to the document.

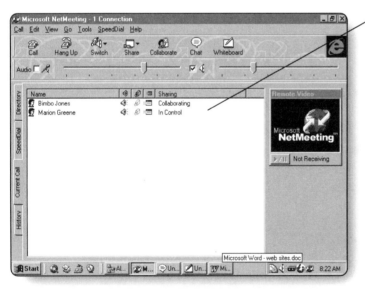

10. **Click anywhere** on your computer screen to take control of the document and make changes. The Current Call tab will be on top and will show who has control of the document.

TRANSFERRING FILES

Transferring files back and forth is perhaps the most popular Internet activity, and doing it through NetMeeting is easy.

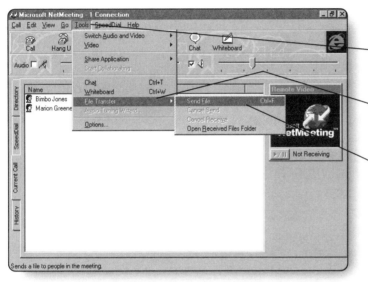

Sending a File

1. Click on **Tools**. The Tools menu will appear.

2. Click on **File Transfer**. A cascading menu will appear.

3. Click on **Send File**. The Select a File to Send dialog box will open.

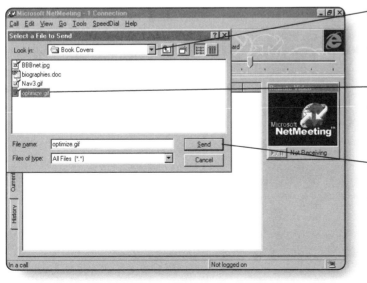

4. Select the **folder** in which the file you want to send is stored. The folder will be selected.

5. Click on the **file** that you want to send. The filename will be selected.

6. Click on **Send**. The file will be sent to the other person in your conference call.

Receiving a File

Receiving a file is a simple process. It mostly involves waiting because you don't want to do anything until the transfer is complete.

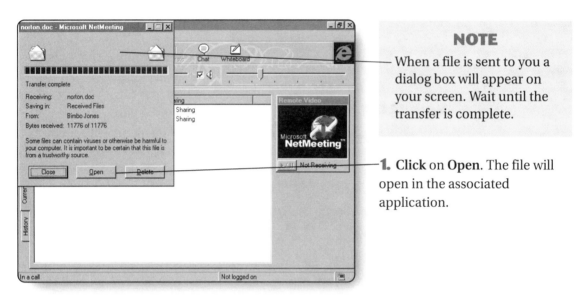

NOTE

When a file is sent to you a dialog box will appear on your screen. Wait until the transfer is complete.

1. **Click** on **Open**. The file will open in the associated application.

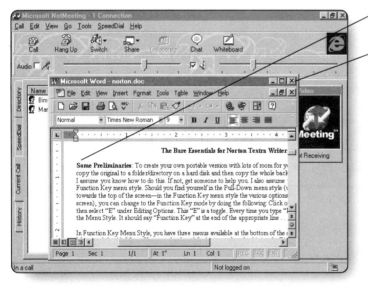

2. **Read** the **document**.

3. **Click** on the application's **Close button** (☒). The file and the application will close.

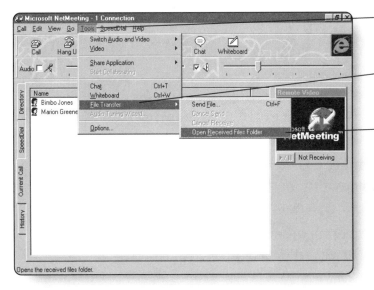

4. Click on **Tools**. The Tools menu will appear.

5. Click on **File Transfer**. A cascading menu will appear.

6. Click on **Open Received Files Folder**. The Received Files Folder will appear.

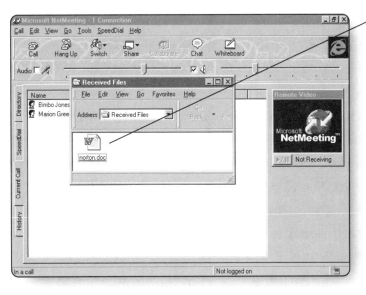

7. Click on the **file**. The file will open in its associated application.

PART V REVIEW QUESTIONS

1. How do you tell NetMeeting to not notify you or answer incoming calls while you are in a conference call? *See "Blocking Incoming Calls" in Chapter 15.*

2. What is one way of finding an address for a person you want to contact for a conference call? *See "Finding More ILS Listings" in Chapter 15.*

3. How can you use NetMeeting to send an e-mail message to someone so that you can schedule a conference call? *See "Sending a Message" in Chapter 15.*

4. What are the two different ways you can connect with another person for a conference call? *See "Connecting to Others" in Chapter 16.*

5. How do you create a speed-dial entry for people you call on a regular basis? *See "Adding a SpeedDial Entry" in Chapter 16.*

6. How do you change the information that is recorded while you are using the NetMeeting chat tool? *See "Changing Chat Options" in Chapter 16.*

7. What are the different kinds of tools that can be used to display information on the whiteboard? *See "Making Your Point With the Whiteboard" in Chapter 16.*

8. Which person in the conference is in control of the shared document? *See "Sharing Applications" in Chapter 17.*

9. How does the person in control allow others in the conference to make changes to the shared document? *See "Sharing Applications" in Chapter 17.*

10. Where does NetMeeting store files that are transferred during a conference call? *See "Receiving a File" in Chapter 17.*

PART VI

Creating a Web Page with FrontPage Express

ush technology"
own—but what e
how Microsoft Int
push technology t
new channels tha

18 What's on the FrontPage Express Screen

Before you dive into FrontPage Express to create your personal Web page, take a little time to get familiar with the program. Spending this time will not only help you get comfortable with the program but also work faster. You may also find out about features of the program that you weren't aware of. In this chapter, you'll learn how to:

✦ Use Wizards to get your Web page started

✦ Create forms

✦ Format text

✦ Move objects around on your Web page

LEARNING FRONTPAGE EXPRESS MENUS

Menus organize all of the functions that FrontPage Express performs into groups. All of the commands within a menu perform functions that are complementary to each other. Inside each menu, commands are divided into groups. The commands within a group perform similar functions or they work in conjunction with each other. The next section takes a look at some fun things you can create with menus.

Getting Started with Wizards

Wizards provide you with a quick and easy start to building a Web page. Each wizard takes you through a series of steps that enable you to customize the Web page to meet your needs and interests. Wizards also help you with Web page design. When you finish the wizard, the beginning of your Web page is displayed. You can then fix up your Web page to include graphics, sounds, animations, and anything else that will give your Web page some class.

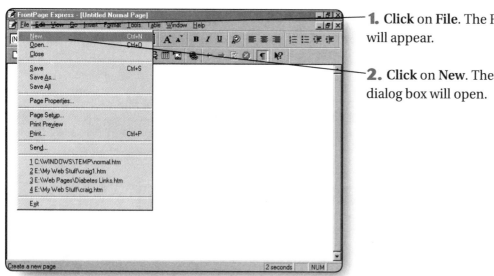

1. **Click** on **File**. The File menu will appear.

2. **Click** on **New**. The New Page dialog box will open.

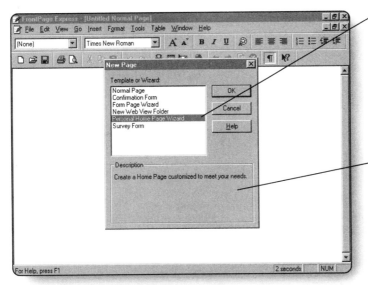

3. **Click** on the **wizard** in the Template or Wizard: box that you want to use to help you build your Web page. The wizard will be selected.

NOTE

When you click on a wizard, a description of what the wizard does will appear in the Description area.

4. **Click** on **OK**. The Wizard will start.

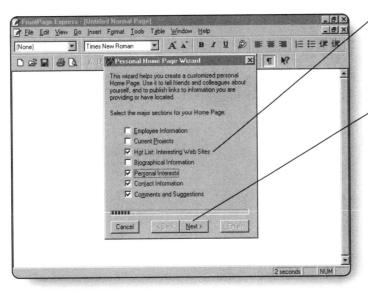

5. **Click** on the **sections** that you want to include in your Web page. A ✔ will appear in the boxes next to those you selected.

6. **Click** on **Next**. The next page of the wizard will appear.

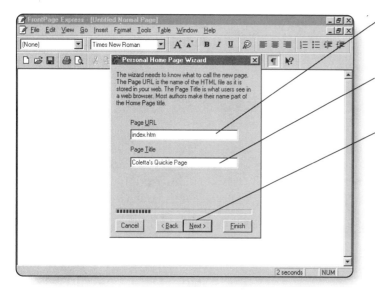

7. Type a **filename** for your Web page in the Page URL text box.

8. Type a **title** for your Web page in the Page Title text box.

9. Click on **Next**. The next page of the wizard will appear.

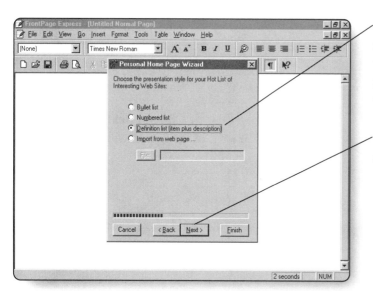

10. Click on the **option button** for the format that you want to use to display your list of favorite Web sites. The option will be selected.

11. Click on **Next**. The next page of the wizard will appear.

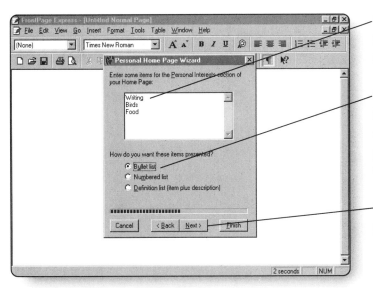

12. Type a list of **personal interest topics** that you want to include on your Web page.

13. Click on the **option button** for the format that you want to use to display your list of personal interests. The option will be selected.

14. Click on **Next**. The next page of the wizard will appear.

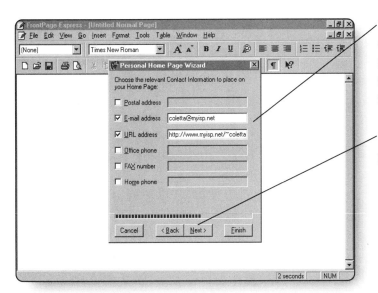

15. Click on the **types of contact information** you want to include in your Web page and type the **corresponding information** in the text box.

16. Click on **Next**. The next page of the wizard will appear.

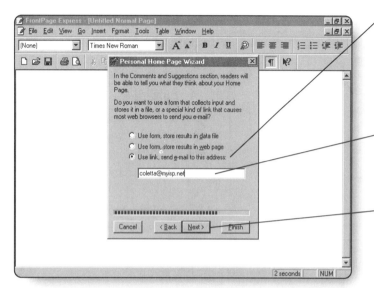

17. **Click** on the **option button** for how you want to use forms to collect information from visitors to your Web page. The option will be selected.

18. **Type** the **e-mail address** in the text box to which responses should be sent.

19. **Click** on **Next**. The next page of the wizard will appear.

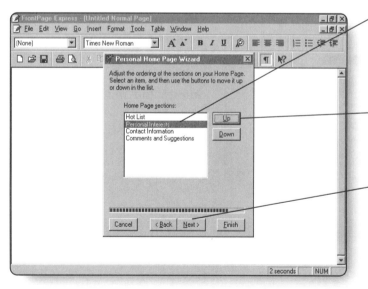

20. **Click** on the **item** in the Home Page sections: box that you want to move. The item will be selected.

21. **Click** on **Up** to move the item up one place in the list. The item will move.

22. **Click** on **Next**. The last page of the wizard will appear.

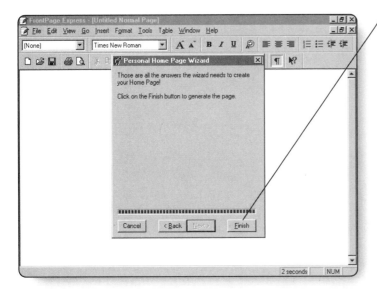

23. **Click** on **Finish**. The wizard will create a beginning format for your personal Web page.

USING THE TOOLBARS

Toolbars provide a quick and easy way of accomplishing the most often used functions of FrontPage Express. Rather than have to search through the menus to find the appropriate command, you can use the buttons right there in front of you. The graphic on each button will give you a pretty good idea of the button's function.

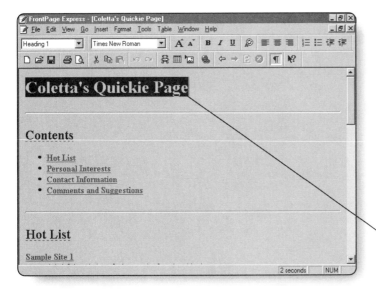

Formatting Text

The Format toolbar is where you go to make your text stand out. You can change the size, shape, and color of text characters. You can turn paragraphs into bulleted or numbered lists. You can also change the alignment of paragraphs to make your words look even better.

1. Select the **text** that you want to format. The text will be highlighted.

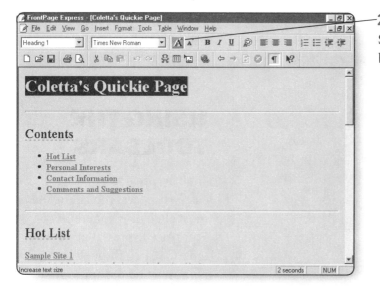

2. **Click** on the **Increase Text Size button**. The text will become larger.

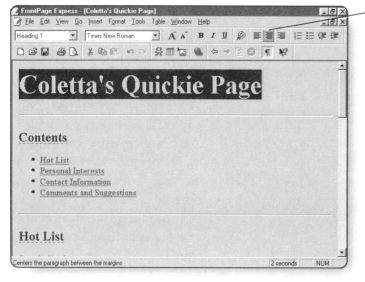

3. **Click** on the **Center button**. The text will be centered between the right and left margins.

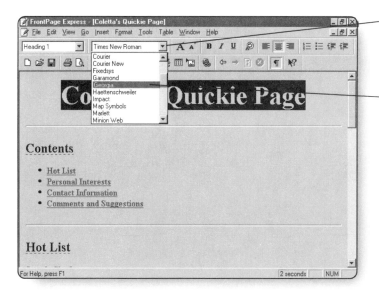

4. **Click** on the **Change Font** drop-down arrow. The Change Font drop-down list will appear.

5. **Click** on a **font**. The name of the font will appear in the Change Font text box and the selected text will change to the new font.

Designing Quick Forms

Forms can be one of the most useful tools available for collecting information.

1. **Place** the **insertion point** on the page where you want to insert the form.

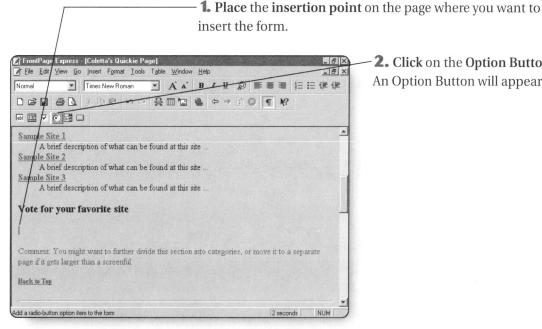

2. **Click** on the **Option Button**. An Option Button will appear.

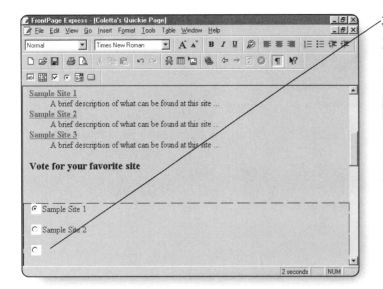

3. **Type text** to describe the purpose of the option button.

4. **Place** the **insertion point** on the page where you want to insert the next button.

5. **Click** on the **Push Button button**. A Push Button will appear.

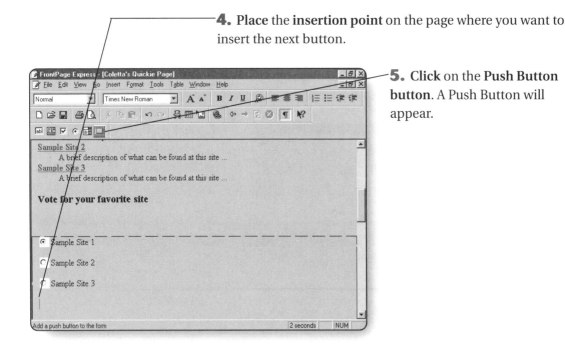

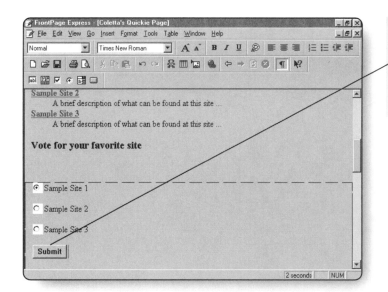

LOOKING AT FRONTPAGE EXPRESS SCREEN ELEMENTS

The following section takes a quick look at screen elements available to you for working with objects and text in FrontPage Express.

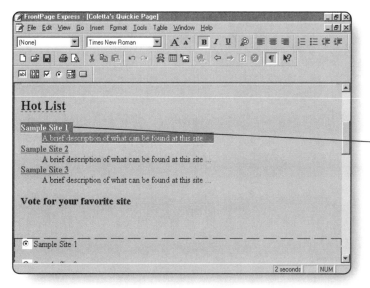

Moving Objects

Objects can be text, pictures, icons, graphics, and other things. To move them around on the screen, follow these steps.

1. **Press** and **hold** the **mouse button** on the text that you want to move and **drag** the **mouse pointer** to the position where you want the text moved. The mouse pointer will change to an arrow with a grayed box attached to it.

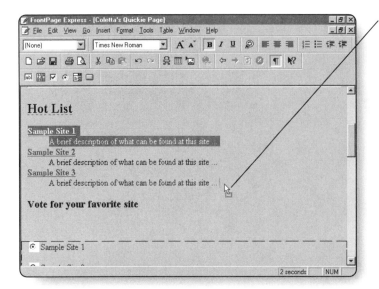

2. **Release** the **mouse button**. The text will appear in its new position.

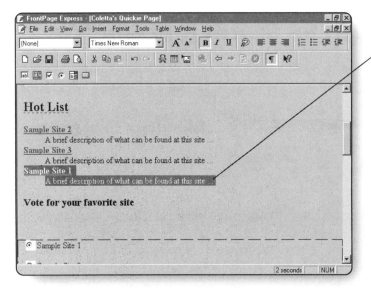

Copying Text

1. **Select** the **text** that you want to copy. The text will be highlighted.

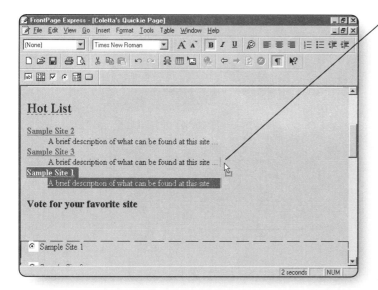

2. Press and hold the right mouse button and drag the text to the place where you want to put the copy of the text. The mouse pointer will change to an arrow with a grayed box attached to it.

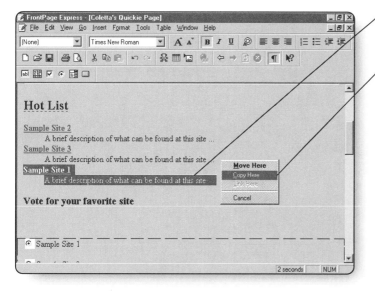

3. Release the mouse button. A menu will appear.

4. Click on Copy Here. The text will be copied to the new position.

19 Creating a Simple Web Page

FrontPage Express is an easy-to-use HTML editor. FrontPage Express allows you to put together simple Web pages while giving you the ability to add a few advanced features to your page. Before you begin building your Web page, you will need to decide what you want your Web page to say and how it should look. This chapter will walk you through creating a simple personal Web page that you can modify later to suit your preferences. In this chapter, you'll learn how to:

✦ Use FrontPage Express to create a personal home page

✦ Add links and graphics

PLACING TEXT ON YOUR PAGE

When you open FrontPage Express, the program will start with a blank page. The cursor is already located at the beginning of the page. You just add some content and do some formatting, and you are ready to get published on the World Wide Web.

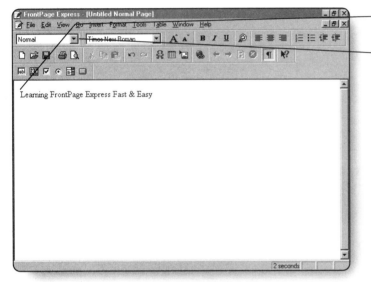

1. **Type** a **title** for your page.

2. **Click** on the **down arrow** (▼) in the Style field. A drop-down list of style options will appear.

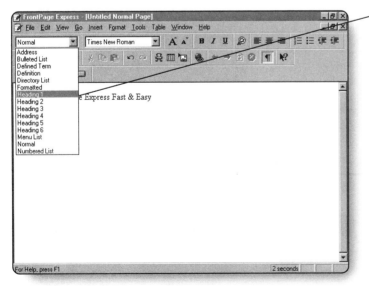

3. **Click** on a **style** that you want to use to make your title stand out from the rest of your text. Your title will appear in the style that you chose.

4. **Press** the **Enter key**. Your cursor will move down to the next line.

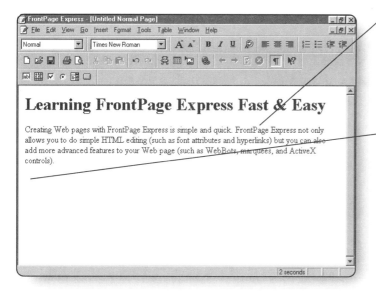

5. Type some **introductory text.** This text is already formatted as Normal style, so you will not need to make any formatting changes.

6. Press the **Enter key.** The cursor will move to a blank line.

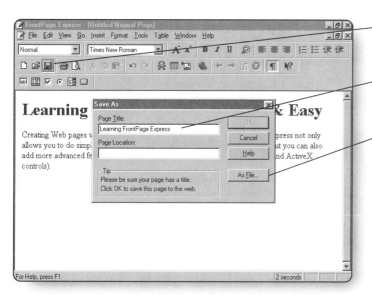

7. Click on the **Save button.** The Save As dialog box will open.

8. Type a **title** for your page in the Page Title: text box.

9. Click on the **As File button** to save the page to your computer. The Save As File dialog box will open.

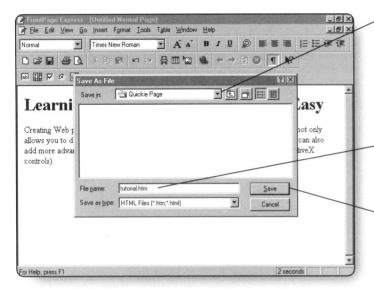

10. **Click** on the **down arrow** (▼) next to the Save in: list box and **choose** the **directory** in which you want to store your Web page. The directory will appear in the Save in: box.

11. **Type** a **filename** for your Web page in the File name: text box.

12. **Click** on **Save**. Your Web page will be stored on your computer's hard drive in the directory that you specified.

TIP

Save your Web page frequently so that you don't lose any of your hard work. Every few minutes, place the mouse pointer over the Save button on the toolbar and click.

ADDING HYPERLINKS

Hyperlinks give visitors to your site an easy way to move around inside your Web site or to jump to another Web site.

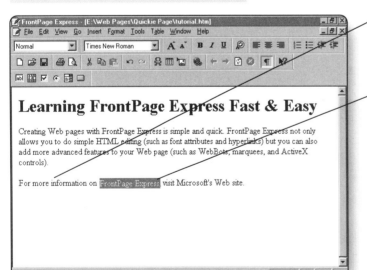

1. **Type** some **text** to describe the Web page to which you will be linking.

2. **Select** the **words** that you want to serve as the hyperlink. The words will be highlighted.

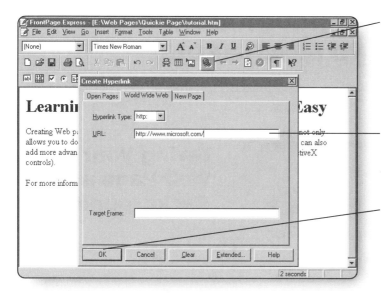

3. **Click** on the **Create or Edit Hyperlink button**. The Create Hyperlink dialog box will open and the World Wide Web tab should be on top.

4. **Type** the **URL**, in the URL: text box, of the Web page to which you want to link.

5. **Click** on **OK**.

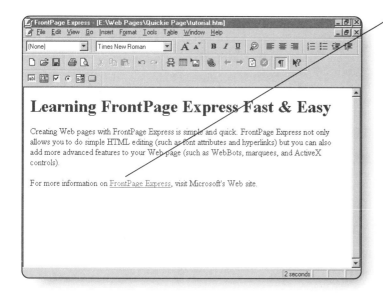

You will be returned to your Web page, and the text that you highlighted will be blue and underlined.

ADDING GRAPHICS AND MULTIMEDIA

Now that you have the basic text for your Web page, it's time to add some graphics.

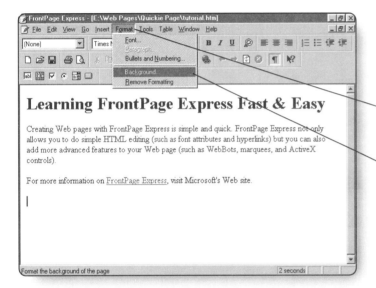

Giving Your Web Page a Background

1. **Click** on **Format**. The Format menu will appear.

2. **Click** on **Background**. The Page Properties dialog box will open, and the Background tab should be on top.

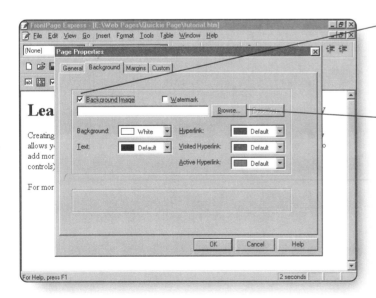

3. **Click** on **Background Image** to add an image as the background. A ✔ will be placed in the box.

4. **Click** on the **Browse button**. The Select Background Image dialog box will open.

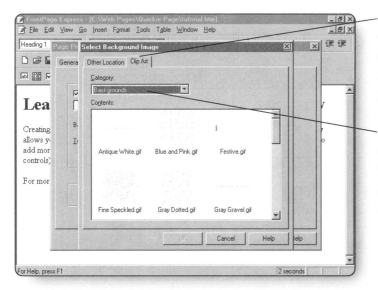

5. **Click** on the **Clip Art tab**. The Clip Art tab will come to the top of the stack with a list of clip art graphics available to FrontPage Express.

6. **Click** on **Backgrounds** in the Category drop-down box. Thumbnail images of all the available backgrounds will appear in the Contents: box.

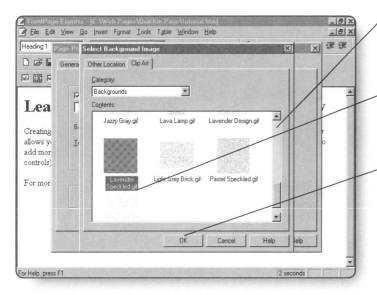

7. **Scroll through** the **list** of backgrounds until you find one you like.

8. **Click** on the **thumbnail image** of the background. The background will be selected.

9. **Click** on **OK**. You will be returned to the Page Properties dialog box.

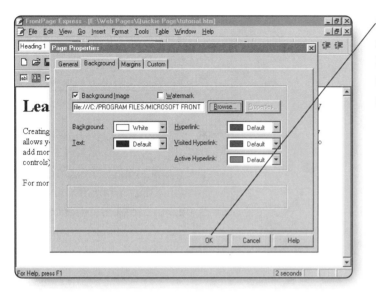

10. **Click** on **OK**. You will be returned to your FrontPage Express Web page. You will be able to see how your background looks on your Web page.

Inserting an Image into Your Web Page

1. **Place** the **cursor** where you want to insert the image.

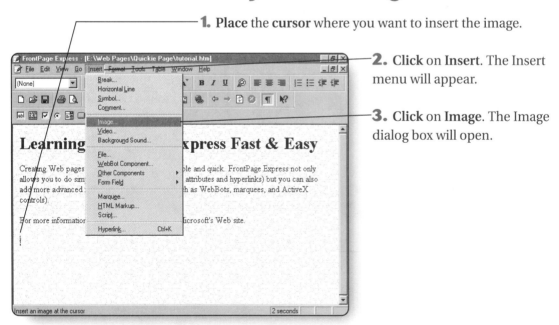

2. **Click** on **Insert**. The Insert menu will appear.

3. **Click** on **Image**. The Image dialog box will open.

4. **Click** on the **Clip Art tab**. The Clip Art tab will come to the top of the stack.

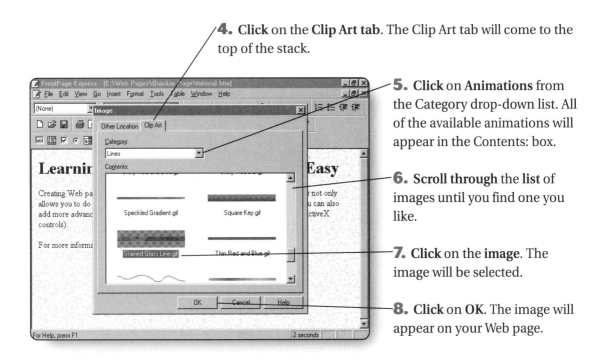

5. **Click** on **Animations** from the Category drop-down list. All of the available animations will appear in the Contents: box.

6. **Scroll through** the **list** of images until you find one you like.

7. **Click** on the **image**. The image will be selected.

8. **Click** on **OK**. The image will appear on your Web page.

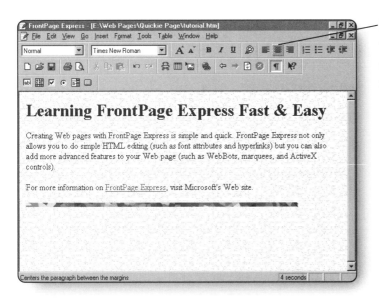

9. **Click** on the **Center button** to center the image on the page, after making sure that the image is selected.

Adding Sound to Your Web Page

1. Click on **Insert**. The Insert menu will appear.

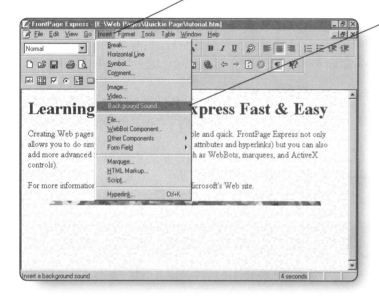

2. Click on **Background Sound**. The Background Sound dialog box will open.

TIP

Your safest bet when adding a background sound to your Web page is to use MIDI format. By using MIDI files, you can be assured that the majority of the people visiting your page will be able to hear your music.

3. Click on the **From File option button**. The option will be selected.

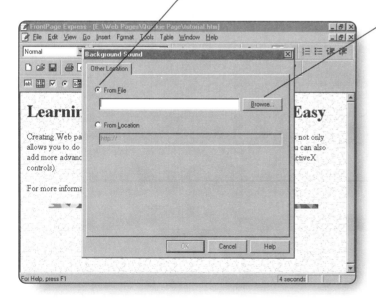

4. Click on **Browse**. The Background Sound dialog box will open.

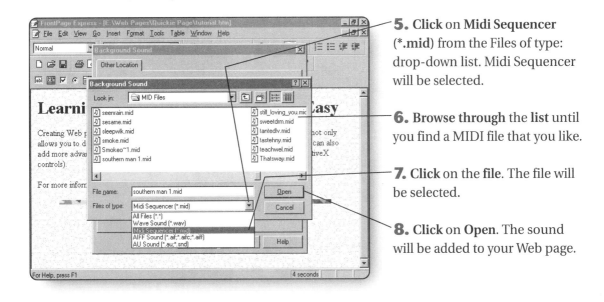

5. Click on **Midi Sequencer (*.mid)** from the Files of type: drop-down list. Midi Sequencer will be selected.

6. Browse through the **list** until you find a MIDI file that you like.

7. Click on the **file**. The file will be selected.

8. Click on **Open**. The sound will be added to your Web page.

9. Click on the **Internet Explorer icon** on your desktop if you want to see how your Web page looks and sounds. The Internet Explorer browser will open.

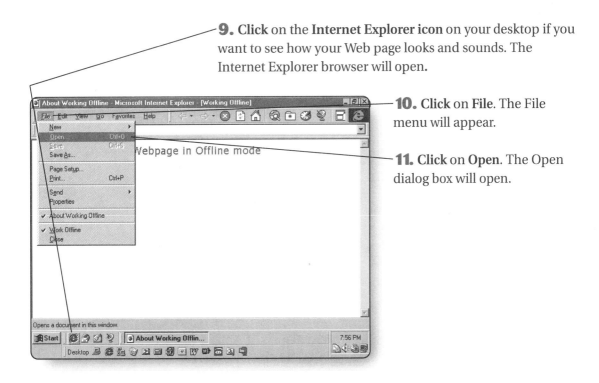

10. Click on **File**. The File menu will appear.

11. Click on **Open**. The Open dialog box will open.

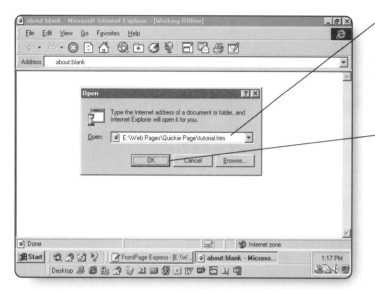

12. **Type** the **path** for the directory and the **filename** where your FrontPage Express Web page is stored in the Open: text box.

13. **Click** on **OK**.

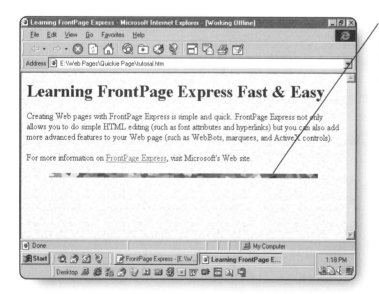

You will be able to see the animated GIF and hear the background sound that you added to your Web page.

PART VI REVIEW QUESTIONS

1. Why should you consider using a wizard to help you get your Web page off to a good start? *See "Getting Started with Wizards" in Chapter 18.*

2. How do you change the way text looks on a Web page? *See "Formatting Text" in Chapter 18.*

3. How do you create a form? *See "Designing Quick Forms" in Chapter 18.*

4. How do you use the mouse to move objects around on your Web page? *See "Moving Objects" in Chapter 18.*

5. How do you use the mouse to copy objects on a Web page? *See "Copying Text" in Chapter 18.*

6. How do you use styles to change the way text is formatted in your Web page? *See "Placing Text on Your Page" in Chapter 19.*

7. How do you save a Web page to your computer? *See "Placing Text on Your Page" in Chapter 19.*

8. How do you create a hyperlink in your Web page? *See "Adding Hyperlinks" in Chapter 19.*

9. How do you add a background to your Web page? *See "Giving Your Web Page a Background" in Chapter 19.*

10. How do you add sound to your Web page that others can hear when they access your page from the Internet? *See "Adding Sound to Your Web Page" in Chapter 19.*

PART VII

Appendix

A Getting Help

If you are new to the Internet and are unfamiliar with using all the software tools that go with it, there are lots of places to turn to for assistance. In this appendix, you'll learn how to:

✦ Get help using the What's This button

✦ Get help using the Help Topics

✦ Get help from Microsoft's Web site

GETTING HELP USING WHAT'S THIS?

As you are working in a program, you will notice the question mark (?) button at the top right corner of the dialog boxes. If you are unsure of what function different options perform, use the What's This button for quick answers.

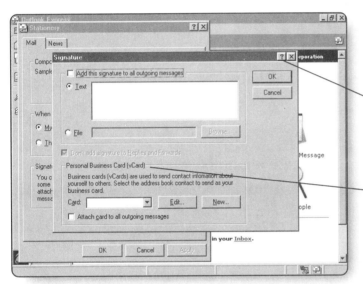

1. **Click** on the **What's This button**. The mouse pointer will change to a pointer with a question mark.

2. **Click** on the **item** that you want more information about. A screen tip will appear.

3. **Click anywhere** outside of the screen tip. The screen tip will disappear and you can continue working with the program.

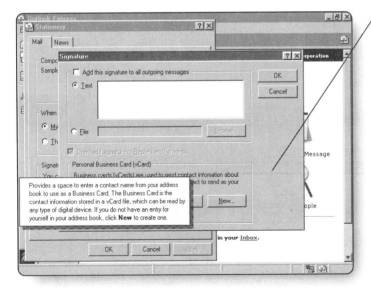

SEARCHING THE HELP FILE

If the What's This button didn't answer your question, it's time to go to the Help topics and search for an answer.

1. **Click** on **Help**. The Help menu will appear.

2. **Click** on **Contents and Index**. The Help Topics dialog box will open.

NOTE

Microsoft has changed the look of the Help files in some Internet Explorer programs. You will notice that Help is contained within a single dialog box. You don't need to navigate between the contents listing and the help topic.

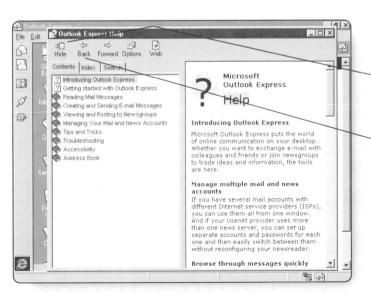

3. **Choose any** of the following actions:

◆ Clicking on the Hide button will hide the Contents and Index section.

◆ Clicking on the Back button will display the previous help topic that you viewed.

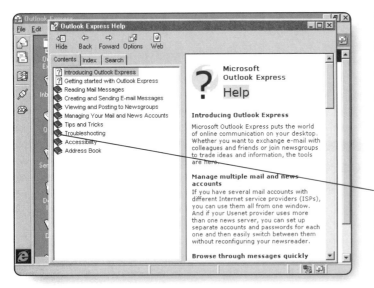

Using the Contents Tab

The Contents tab reads somewhat like the table of contents of a book. You may have to hunt for a while to find the answer you need.

1. **Click** on the **Book icon** next to the topic that you want to know more about. The topic will expand to show the contents.

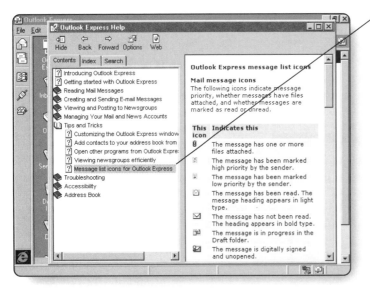

2. **Click** on the **item** that you need help with. The help topic will appear in the right frame.

Using the Index Tab

The Index dialog box looks something like the index that you find in the backs of books. You can either scroll through the list to find the topic you are looking for or you can type some keywords to reduce your search time.

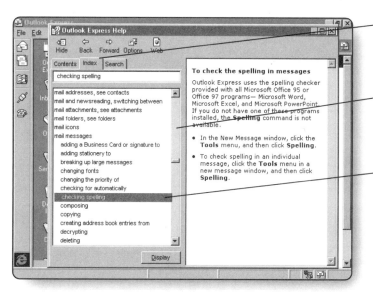

1. Click on the **Index tab**. The list of help topics will appear in the left frame of the dialog box.

2. Scroll through the **list** of topics to find the topic that you need help with.

3. Double-click on the **topic**. The help file for the topic will appear in the right frame.

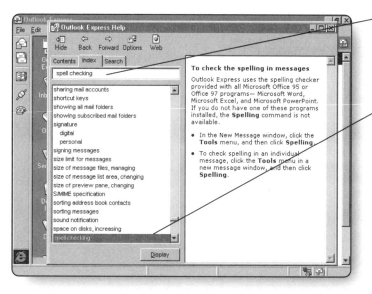

4. Type keywords in the text box for the subject you need help with. The closest match will display in the list of topics.

5. Click on the **topic** that is the closest match. The help topic for that item will appear in the right frame.

Using the Find Tab

Some Internet Explorer programs still use the old Microsoft method of displaying help files. For these programs, you can still use Find for a more precise search.

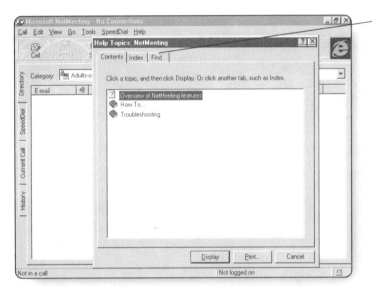

1. **Click** on the **Find tab**. The Find Setup Wizard will start.

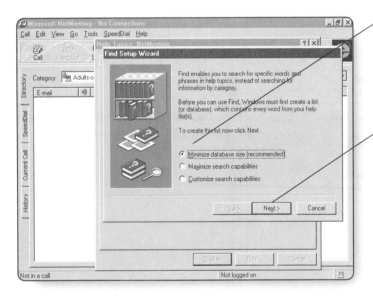

2. **Click** on an **option button** for the size database that you want to create to use in your search. The option will be selected.

3. **Click** on Next. The help database will be created.

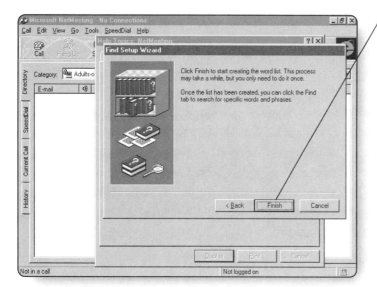

4. **Click** on **Finish**. The Find dialog box will open.

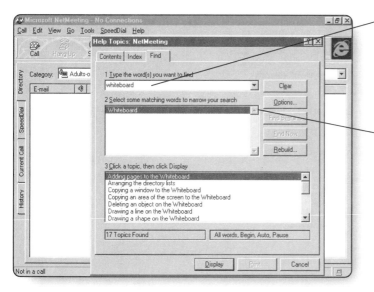

5. **Type** a **keyword** to describe the topic that you need help with. Matching words will appear in the second section of the dialog box.

6. **Click** on a **matching word** that comes closest to describing what you need help with. The number of available topics will narrow down in the third section of the dialog box to match your help needs more closely.

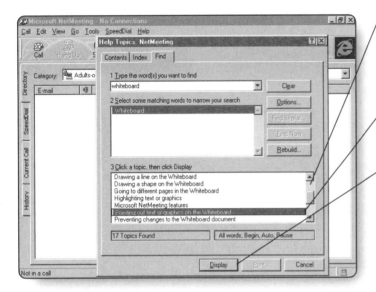

7. **Scroll through** the list of topics in the third section of the dialog box until you find one that answers your questions.

8. **Click** on the **topic**. The topic will be selected.

9. **Click** on **Display**. The help topic will appear in a separate window.

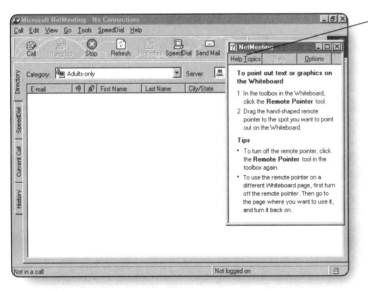

10. **Click** on **Help Topics**. You will be returned to the Find dialog box.

GETTING HELP ON THE WEB

Microsoft provides a wealth of information on its Web site. If the program's help files haven't answered your questions, it's time to get online and give Microsoft a call.

1. **Click** on **Help**. The Help menu will appear.

2. **Click** on **Online Support**. The Internet Explorer Support Home Page will appear.

3. **Type a keyword** to describe the topic that you need help with.

NOTE

If your help need is not specific to Internet Explorer, click to insert a ✔ in the box next to Search entire Support Site to search the entire Microsoft support site.

4. **Click** on **Find**. Your search query will be sent to the Microsoft Technical Support server, and a Security Alert warning box will appear.

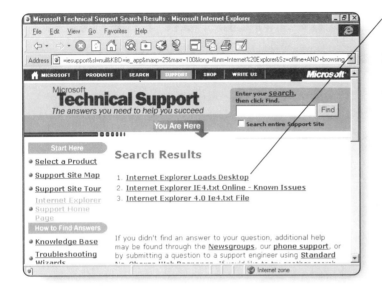

5. **Click** on the **search result** that is the closest match to your help needs. The associated help topic will appear in the browser window.

Glossary

3-D. A visual effect that makes images appear to have depth.

A

Address bar. An area where you can type the URL address of the Web page you want to access. With AutoComplete, it isn't always necessary to type the whole URL address; the browser can do some of that for you. You can also perform searches from the address bar.

Animated GIF. A type of GIF image that combines several images into a single file. When the GIF image is viewed, the images display in a continuous cycle, like you would see when watching a cartoon. GIF animation doesn't give the same level of control and flexibility as other animation formats. It is popular because animated GIFs can be viewed in any Web browser and the file size is small.

Anonymous FTP. A file transfer method that allows users to access a server without the need of a password. Usually, you would log in as anonymous and use your e-mail address as a password.

Applet. A small Java program that runs in a Web page. Java applets can take a long time to download to your computer.

AU. Audio. The most common file format for transmitting sound over the Internet. If you want to play .au files that you find on the Internet, you will need a special audio player.

Authentication. The process of identifying an individual, usually based on a username and password. Authentication merely ensures that the individual is who he or she claims to be, but says nothing about the access rights of the individual.

AutoComplete. A feature used in the Address bar that suggests possible URL addresses based on the text that you are typing.

AutoSearch. A feature used in the Address bar that performs a search based on words you provide. Type go, find, or ?, type a search word, and press the Enter key.

B

Browser. A software program that is needed to navigate Web pages and FTP sites on the Internet.

Business Card. The entry in the Windows Address Book that contains your contact information. A Business Card entry contains your name and e-mail address. You can also add your home address and phone number, the URL address for your personal Web page, your business address and phone number, and the URL address for your business.

C

Cable modem. A modem that operates over cable TV lines. Cable TV lines have a greater bandwidth than telephone lines that would allow for faster access to the Internet when connected through a cable modem. This is new technology that is still developing. There are a couple of hurdles that need to be overcome before cable modem connection to the Internet can be made widespread.

Carpal tunnel syndrome. A common occupational hazard of intense Web surfers. Carpal tunnel syndrome occurs when the same small movements are repeated over and over. When you start experiencing numbness or burning in the fingers or wrist, you will need to make some changes in your computer workspace. Make sure your chair and keyboard are at the correct height. You may want to consider replacing your mouse with a graphics tablet. Also, take frequent breaks from typing.

Certificate Authority. A trusted third-party organization or company that issues digital certificates used to create digital signatures and public-private key pairs. The role of the Certificate Authority is to guarantee that the individual granted the certificate is, in fact, who they claim to be.

Channels. Web sites that are automatically updated and downloaded to your computer on a schedule specified by the channel content provider.

Compression. A method of squeezing a file into a smaller size. Compressed files transfer much more quickly.

Content Advisor. A feature of Internet Explorer and its components that give you the control over the type of content that your computer can access on the Internet. By using the Content Advisor, you can set up your Internet Explorer suite programs so that Web sites, newsgroups, and chat rooms that are offensive to you can not be accessed from your computer.

Cookie. A piece of information that a Web server stores on your computer until it's time for the server to read it. For example, a cookie that is made while you shop around a Web mall contains a list of the items you're planning to purchase. This way you can leave the Web site and save your list of items so that you can resume your shopping spree next time you return to the mall.

Cross-posting. The practice of posting a message to more than one newsgroup. This is only proper netiquette if the topic is of interest in more than one newsgroup.

D

Dial-up. A type of Internet connection established when you dial a number through your computer's modem to connect to your ISP.

Digital certificate. An attachment to an e-mail message used to keep the contents of the message secure. Digital certificates are used to verify that a user sending a message is who they claim to be, and to provide the receiver with the means to encode a reply. An individual wishing to send an encrypted message applies for a digital certificate from a Certificate Authority. The Certificate Authority issues an encrypted digital certificate containing the applicant's public key. The recipient of the encrypted message uses the Certificate Authority's public key to decode the digital certificate attached to the message.

Digitizing tablet. An electronic board that detects the movement of a pen or a cursor that enables you to enter drawings and sketches into a computer. The cursor is similar to a mouse except that it has a

window with cross hairs for pinpoint placement and has as many as 16 buttons. A pen looks like a ballpoint pen but uses an electronic head instead of ink. Most digitizing tablets support mouse emulation mode where the pen or cursor acts like a mouse.

Directory services. Search tools that you can use to find the e-mail and postal addresses for individuals and businesses. There are several directory services that you can use and that can be accessed from the Windows Address Book.

Dynamic HTML. A new programming language that creates Web pages that are interactive and do not require long transfer times between your computer and the server. Dynamic HTML can change the way elements look without refreshing the browser window, change the objects that appear in the browser window without having to access the server for the object, animate objects on a Web page, and build forms that are interactive and can be processed faster.

E

E-mail. Electronic mail. Electronic correspondence system where messages are sent over a network such as the Internet.

Explorer bar. A new feature in Internet Explorer that allows you to see your list of favorites, search results, channels, or history in a frame in the browser window while still allowing you to view Web pages.

F

FAQ. Frequently Asked Questions. A list of questions on a particular subject that answers questions most often asked by new users. Before asking questions in a newsgroup, read the newsgroup's FAQ and see if your question has already been answered.

Favorite. A URL address stored in the Internet Explorer browser that can be accessed easily from the Favorites menu or the Favorites button. You can add more than just Web sites to your list of Favorites. You can also add newsgroups and chat rooms.

Flame. To send a message that is hostile, rude, or some other inappropriate behavior.

Forms. A method used in Web pages to collect data from visitors to the Web site.

Frame. A method of dividing the browser display area into separate sections, each of which is really a different Web page.

FTP. File Transfer Protocol. A method of sending and receiving computer files over the Internet.

Full duplex. The transmission of data in two directions simultaneously. When you talk on the telephone, you are using full-duplex device because both parties can talk at the same time. When using full-duplex, the data that is transmitted does not appear on your screen until it has been received and sent back by the other party. This ensures that the data has been transmitted correctly.

G

GIF. Graphics Interchange Format. A file format that compresses computer generated images in order to prepare them to be viewed in Web pages.

H

Half duplex. The transmission of data in one direction at a time. When using half-duplex, each character that is transmitted appears immediately on your screen. This is called local echo because the characters are echoed by the local device.

History list. A list of all the URLs that were visited during an Internet session. You can use the History list to return to a page you visited previously during your Internet session.

HTML. Hypertext Markup Language. One of the common languages used to create Web pages.

Hyperlink. Text that is usually underlined that you can click on to access another Web page or an FTP server.

Hypermedia. The use of hypertext, images, sound, video, animation, and other media in a Web page.

I

Image map. A graphical image that has several hyperlinks contained in it.

Inbox Assistant. Manages your incoming e-mail. The Inbox Assistant can automatically sort messages into folders, forward messages to people you specify, or delete messages that you don't want to see.

Internet. A global computer network where users can share files, exchange e-mail, converse in newsgroups, and view Web pages.

ISP. Internet Service Provider. A company that provides Internet access for its customers.

J

JPEG. Joint Photographic Experts' Group. A file format that compresses photographic images in order to prepare them to be viewed in Web pages.

Jump. To move from one Web page to another using hyperlinks.

L

Lurker. A person who reads newsgroup postings, but rarely joins in the discussion. When you visit a newsgroup for the first time, you are encouraged to lurk until you have a feel for how the newsgroup operates.

M

Marquee. Information that scrolls across the screen in a Web page.

MIDI. Musical Instrument Digital Interface. A file format used to store music.

MIME. Multipurpose Internet Mail Extension. A method for sending non-textual data, such as audio files and graphic images, as encoded attachments to e-mail messages.

MPEG. Motion Picture Experts Group. A file format for high-quality video compression.

N

Netiquette. Techie-speak for Internet etiquette. This is the informal code of manners that governs online conduct.

Newsgroup. A discussion forum on the Internet.

Newsgroup filters. Allow you to specify the types of newsgroup messages that you do not want to view. The filter prevents the message from being downloaded to your computer and from displaying the header information in the list of messages.

Noise. Interference in the telephone line that destroys the integrity of data signals. Noise comes from a variety of sources such as radio waves, electrical wires, lightning, and bad connections. One of the advantages of fiber optic cables is that they are much less susceptible to noise.

O

Offline browsing. Being able to view Web pages without being connected to your ISP or the Internet. You would use offline browsing if you don't want to tie up the phone line or if you don't have access to the Internet. You must download Web pages to your computer before you can view them offline.

Online session. The time you spend on the Internet. The session begins when you connect to your ISP, it includes everything you do from lurking through newsgroups to downloading files from an FTP server, and ends when you hang up.

P

Personal certificate. This stores information about you, usually a name and password, and it is used when you access a site that needs verification of your identity.

Postmaster. The person who makes sure that the electronic mail always gets delivered for a domain. The postmaster also handles complaints against mail accounts in that domain. If someone is using the Internet inappropriately, send an e-mail to postmaster@domain.com.

Profile assistant. Stores information about you that you have supplied and allows you to share this information with Web sites that need this information. You will no longer need to re-type this information every time you visit a Web site. This information cannot be used by others without your permission.

Protocol. A set of rules and standards that allow computers to transfer information.

R

Restricted sites zone. A security zone that contains sites from which you do not want to download files because you feel that the downloaded content could damage your computer.

S

ScreenTip. A Windows Help feature that displays a flag description onscreen when the mouse is held over a screen element.

Scrollbar. A Windows screen element that is used in conjunction with the mouse to move to different areas of a page.

Search engine. A program that searches a database of Web pages and other Internet resources. When you request information on a subject, the search engine returns a list of possible matches.

Security certificate. A file on your computer that is used as an identification for you in Internet commerce.

Security zones. A new feature in Internet Explorer and its components. This feature allows you to specify the type of content that can be downloaded to your computer based on the zone the Web site falls into.

Start page. The Web page that first appears when you open the Internet Explorer browser. You can set the start page to be any page that you want. It can be a page from a Web site you visit often, a blank page, or a page that is stored on your computer's hard drive.

Stationery. A feature of Outlook Express that makes creating HTML messages a snap. There are several stationery styles that are installed with Outlook Express. Each style contains a background that sets the theme and a text style that complements the background. You can design your own stationery to use in Outlook Express.

Streaming. A technique for transferring data so that it can be processed as a steady and continuous stream. Streaming technologies are becoming increasingly important with the growth of the Internet because most users do not have fast enough access to download large multimedia files quickly. With streaming, the client browser or plug-in can start displaying the data before the entire file has been transmitted.

Subscriptions. Allows you to set a schedule to have the Internet Explorer browser automatically check to see if a Web site has been updated.

T

TCP/IP. Transmission Control Protocol/Internet Protocol. The predominant method used to manage communication over the Internet.

Telecommuting. Jack Nilles first used this term in the early 1970s to describe a work environment where workers can work at home and transmit data and documents to a central office via telephone lines. The growth of the Internet has made telecommuting possible for many people. There are many benefits to telecommuting. Telecommuting is one way to save our earth's resources. It also allows families to spend more time together. But, telecommuting is not appropriate for every occupation or individual.

Text mode. A browser view that displays text only. You cannot view graphic images, VRML, or sound while in text mode.

Thread. The list of replies to an e-mail or newsgroup message. Threads allow you to follow the flow of messages in a conversation topic. As you read through a thread, you will read messages as they were posted to the newsgroup and according to which message they are responding.

Trusted sites zone. A security zone that contains sites that you believe you can download files from and not have to worry about the downloaded content damaging your computer.

U

URL. Uniform Resource Locator. A standardized method of identifying a Web page on the Internet. URLs consist of a service, the domain, and a directory path.

Usenet. An Internet service that provides approximately 15,000 discussion forums that are open to the Internet public.

V

Videoconferencing. Conducting a conference between two or more people who are located at different sites by using a computer network to transmit audio and video data. Each person has a video camera, microphone, and speakers attached to their computer. Voices, video, and data are carried over the network and delivered to other people's computers.

Virtual reality. An artificial environment created with computer hardware and software. The virtual reality environment appears and feels like a real environment. To "enter" a virtual reality, you wear special gloves, earphones, and goggles. These devices receive their input from the computer system. In addition to feeding sensory input to you, the devices also monitor your actions. The goggles track how your eyes move and respond accordingly by sending new video input. One caution about virtual reality: After 30 minutes in a virtual reality environment, you will feel as though you have a blood alcohol level of .1.

VRML. Virtual Reality Modeling Language. A World Wide Web specification for displaying 3-dimensional objects. VRML produces a 3-dimensional space that appears on your screen. And you can move within this space by pressing keys to turn left or right, up or down, or forward or backward. The images change, giving you the impression that you are moving through a real space. To view VRML files you need a VRML browser or a VRML plug-in to a Web browser.

W

Web site certificate. This guarantees the identify of a secure Web site, making sure that no other Web site assumes its identity.

Webcasting. Using the World Wide Web to broadcast information. Unlike typical surfing, which relies on a pull method of transferring Web pages, webcasting uses push technologies. One of the first webcasting services is PointCast. Microsoft and Netscape are developing their own webcasting products and services.

Webmaster. The person responsible for maintaining a Web site.

World Wide Web. A system of hypertext documents (Web pages) that can be accessed over the Internet.

Index

Send Us
YOUR COMMENTS

Dear Reader:

Thank you for buying this book. In order to offer you more quality books on the topics *you* would like to see, we need your input. At Prima Publishing, we pride ourselves on timely responsiveness to our readers needs. If you'll complete and return this brief questionnaire, **we will listen!**

Name: (first) _____ (M.I.) _____ (last) _____

Company: _____ Type of business: _____

Address: _____ City: _____ State: _____ Zip: _____

Phone: _____ Fax: _____ E-mail address: _____

May we contact you for research purposes? ❏ Yes ❏ No

(If you participate in a research project, we will supply you with your choice of a book from Prima Tech)

❶ How would you rate this book, overall?

❏ Excellent ❏ Fair
❏ Very Good ❏ Below Average
❏ Good ❏ Poor

❷ Why did you buy this book?

❏ Price of book ❏ Content
❏ Author's reputation ❏ Prima's reputation
❏ CD-ROM/disk included with book
❏ Information highlighted on cover
❏ Other (Please specify): _____

❸ How did you discover this book?

❏ Found it on bookstore shelf
❏ Saw it in Prima Publishing catalog
❏ Recommended by store personnel
❏ Recommended by friend or colleague
❏ Saw an advertisement in: _____
❏ Read book review in: _____
❏ Saw it on Web site: _____
❏ Other (Please specify): _____

❹ Where did you buy this book?

❏ Bookstore (name) _____
❏ Computer Store (name) _____
❏ Electronics Store (name) _____
❏ Wholesale Club (name) _____
❏ Mail Order (name) _____
❏ Direct from Prima Publishing
❏ Other (please specify): _____

❺ Which computer periodicals do you read regularly? _____

_____

_____

_____

❻ Would you like to see your name in print?

May we use your name and quote you in future Prima Publishing books or promotional materials?

❏ Yes ❏ No

❼ Comments & Suggestions: _____

_____

_____

PRIMA TECH

---

8 Where do you use your computer?

Work	❑ 100%	❑ 75%	❑ 50%	❑ 25%
Home	❑ 100%	❑ 75%	❑ 50%	❑ 25%
School	❑ 100%	❑ 75%	❑ 50%	❑ 25%

Other _____

9 How do you rate your level of computer skills?

❑ Beginner
❑ Advanced
❑ Intermediate

10 What is your age?

❑ Under 18
❑ 18-24   ❑ 40-49
❑ 25-29   ❑ 50-59
❑ 30-39   ❑ 60-over

11 I would be interested in computer books on these topics

❑ Word Processing   ❑ Database:
❑ Networking   ❑ Spreadsheets
❑ Desktop Publishing ❑ Web site design

Other_____

SAVE A STAMP ——————————————

Visit our Web Site at: **www.prima-tech.com/comments**
and simply fill in one of our online Response Forms

OTHER BOOKS FROM PRIMA PUBLISHING

ISBN	Title	Price
0-7615-1363-9	Access 97 Fast & Easy	$16.99
0-7615-1412-0	ACT! 4.0 Fast & Easy	$16.99
0-7615-1348-5	Create FrontPage 98 Web Pages In a Weekend	$24.99
0-7615-1294-2	Create PowerPoint Presentations In a Weekend	$19.99
0-7615-1388-4	Create Your First Web Page In a Weekend, Revised Edition	$24.99
0-7615-0428-1	The Essential Excel 97 Book	$27.99
0-7615-0733-7	The Essential Netscape Communicator Book	$24.99
0-7615-0969-0	The Essential Office 97 Book	$27.99
0-7615-0695-0	The Essential Photoshop Book	$35.00
0-7615-1182-2	The Essential PowerPoint 97 Book	$24.99
0-7615-1136-9	The Essential Publisher 97 Book	$24.99
0-7615-0967-4	The Essential Windows 98 Book	$24.99
0-7615-0752-3	The Essential Windows NT 4 Book	$27.99
0-7615-0427-3	The Essential Word 97 Book	$27.99
0-7615-0425-7	The Essential WordPerfect 8 Book	$24.99
0-7615-1008-7	Excel 97 Fast & Easy	$16.99
0-7615-1534-8	FrontPage 98 Fast & Easy	$16.99
0-7615-1194-6	Increase Your Web Traffic In a Weekend	$19.99
0-7615-1191-1	Internet Explorer 4.0 Fast & Easy	$19.99
0-7615-1137-7	Jazz Up Your Web Site In a Weekend	$24.99
0-7615-1379-5	Learn Access 97 In a Weekend	$19.99
0-7615-1293-4	Learn HTML In a Weekend	$24.99
0-7615-1295-0	Learn the Internet In a Weekend	$19.99
0-7615-1217-9	Learn Publisher 97 In a Weekend	$19.99
0-7615-1251-9	Learn Word 97 In a Weekend	$19.99
0-7615-1296-9	Learn Windows 98 In a Weekend	$19.99
0-7615-1193-8	Lotus 1-2-3 97 Fast & Easy	$16.99
0-7615-1420-1	Managing with Microsoft Project 98	$29.99
0-7615-1382-5	Netscape Navigator 4.0 Fast & Easy	$16.99
0-7615-1162-8	Office 97 Fast & Easy	$16.99
0-7615-1186-5	Organize Your Finances with Quicken Deluxe 98 In a Weekend	$19.99
0-7615-1405-8	Outlook 98 Fast & Easy	$16.99
0-7615-1677-8	Prima's Official Companion to Family Tree Maker 5	$24.99
0-7615-1513-5	Publisher 98 Fast & Easy	$19.99
0-7615-1699-9	SmartSuite Millennium Fast & Easy	$16.99
0-7615-1138-5	Upgrade Your PC In a Weekend	$19.99
0-7615-1328-0	Web Advertising and Marketing, 2nd Edition	$34.95
1-55958-738-5	Windows 95 Fast & Easy	$19.95
0-7615-1006-0	Windows 98 Fast & Easy	$16.99
0-7615-1007-9	Word 97 Fast & Easy	$16.99
0-7615-1316-7	Word 97 for Law Firms	$29.99
0-7615-1083-4	WordPerfect 8 Fast & Easy	$16.99
0-7615-1188-1	WordPerfect Suite 8 Fast & Easy	$16.99

To Order Books

Please send me the following items:

Quantity	Title	Unit Price	Total
_____	_____	$ _____	$ _____
_____	_____	$ _____	$ _____
_____	_____	$ _____	$ _____
_____	_____	$ _____	$ _____
_____	_____	$ _____	$ _____

Subtotal $ _____

Deduct 10% when ordering 3-5 books $ _____

7.25% Sales Tax (CA only) $ _____

8.25% Sales Tax (TN only) $ _____

5.0% Sales Tax (MD and IN only) $ _____

7.0% G.S.T. Tax (Canada only) $ _____

Shipping and Handling* $ _____

Total Order $ _____

*Shipping and Handling depend on Subtotal.

Subtotal	Shipping/Handling
$0.00–$14.99	$3.00
$15.00–$29.99	$4.00
$30.00–$49.99	$6.00
$50.00–$99.99	$10.00
$100.00–$199.99	$13.50
$200.00+	Call for Quote

Foreign and all Priority Request orders:
Call Order Entry department
for price quote at 916-632-4400

This chart represents the total retail price of books only
(before applicable discounts are taken).

By Telephone: With American Express, MC or Visa,
call 800-632-8676 or 916-632-4400. Mon–Fri, 8:30-4:30.

www.prima-tech.com

By E-mail: sales@primapub.com

By Mail: Just fill out the information below and send with your remittance to:

P
PRIMA TECH

Prima Publishing
P.O. Box 1260BK
Rocklin, CA 95677

My name is _____

I live at _____

City_____ State _____ ZIP _____

MC/Visa#_____ Exp._____

Check/money order enclosed for $ _____ Payable to Prima Publishing

Daytime telephone _____

Signature _____